USA and RACIAL DIVIDE

Lord Heal Me and Heal Our Land

Dr. Margaret Gray Robinson

ISBN 978-1-64471-229-0 (Paperback)
ISBN 978-1-64471-230-6 (Digital)

Covenant Books, Inc.
11661 Hwy 707
Murrells Inlet, SC 29576
www.covenantbooks.com

Contents

Preface

"It cannot be accomplished by the marches of the 1960s, but by a spiritual revolution." These were the words that I heard in 2012. However, it took five years for me to understand what those words meant. Within those five years, I encountered many attacks of the enemy to hinder the writing of this book. After careful examination of my life for the last sixty-two years, the urgency to complete this book only increased as I contemplated the people (like myself), that may be silently dying inside. Since childhood, I had inquired of God why the reality of my life was so different from the truth of God's Word.

As an African American woman, born in the south in the mid-1950s, the love of God was not something that I saw or experienced. Maybe I was looking in the wrong place or at the wrong thing. Although I read about God's love for me, the world around me showed everything but love. I had managed to bury my disappointments deep inside me, knowing that in the church world, it was not wise to admit your hurts.

In a dream many years ago, I had envisioned many soldiers on a battlefield. The soldiers were losing the war because each soldier was wounded in some way. In the dream, I noticed that each soldier hid the limb that was wounded so that other soldiers could not see that they were wounded. The refusal to acknowledge a need for help left the entire company of soldiers open for the enemy to destroy. No one wanted to admit that they needed help. This is what is happening in lives around the world. As we suffer silently, the enemy is destroying families, nations, and our world. The United States of America and the Body of Christ needs help!

The hurts that I had buried so many decades ago had festered inside, and the emptiness only grew deeper, impacting every area of my life. I had buried the hurts deep down on the inside until it began to fester and smell like an open sore. I tried to forgive and be healed, but the continued hurts, disappointments, unfulfilled promises, and broken dreams aggravated the wounds that had never been healed. Therefore, it became like an open wound with salt poured into it. Eventually, like a volcano erupts, spreading hot lava with hot ash (destroying everything in its path), the venom of bitterness, hatred, unforgiveness, anger, resentment, and entitlement destroyed everyone I met, including myself and those that I loved. I guess it's true: "hurting people, hurt people."

But at some point, even hurting people must decide to look beyond themselves and accept healing so that they can be a blessing to others. February 2012 brought those hurts back to the surface when Trayvon Martin, a young, teenage African American boy, was shot and killed in Florida. Why had this been so traumatic for me? After all, it was nothing unusual for an African American to be murdered for merely being a person of color. Whether by lynching, an undeserved bullet, systems of discrimination, or black-on-black crime, it's all murder. Despite the frustration and pain that I had felt since childhood, I still loved God more than life itself. However, I needed answers to this problem that had plagued our world my entire life. Answers that would require me to dig deeper into the root cause of color bias in our nation and the world.

As I approached the history behind mankind from God's perspective, I begin to better understand my world and the people in it. My heart began to soften as I began to understand what had happened, what was happening now, and what would continue to happen unless the hearts of men changed.

This book uncovers racism at its core and seeks to provide an answer for those who truly love God and desire to do things His way. For those who feel that their opinion is better than God's word, this book will still serve as an opportunity for self-examination. For a detailed description of experiences that led to this book, please read my novel entitled *Struggle Without: Struggle Within.*

Introduction

I have often wondered why many of God's people seldom experience the fullness of God's blessings. I had become acquainted with racism in 1965 at age ten. It was at this age that I became aware that the world's view of my dark skin was not in line with what God said about me. Nothing about the world's view, or future similar experiences, matched what I learned at age six about Jesus and His love for me. My reality really did not look like love, and my little mind couldn't see the love of God in any of these experiences.

Since that day, I have been in search of my true identity not from the world's viewpoint, nor tradition or religion, but from God's perspective. That quest for truth has led to fifty-two years of God's performing one surgical procedure after another on my heart. Looking back over the last fifty-two years, I realize that certain experiences from childhood had left an imprint on my psyche that has impacted every area of my life (read my novel on *Struggle Without: Struggle Within*). Seeking healing and wholeness for myself and others, I became aware that healing could never occur until I got to the root of my problem. If I continued to hide my sorrows and pain, the enemy would continue his harassment and oppression.

As I pondered over my life and the current-day string of police shootings, my mind went back to those horrifying days of KKK rallies, headlines of lynchings, and white men in suits spewing out words of hatred all because of the color of a person's skin. Despite the gloom of those days, there were people of all races who brought light while risking their own lives. These were foot soldiers—some known, others behind the scene, but all making a difference in the lives of people around the world. Now my heart wondered, *How could these people who gave their lives [many as unsung heroes] fathom how we could, after fifty-two years, be back at this same road again?*

It then dawned on me that the cycle was never completed. Laws of the 1960s were enacted that forced men to do the "right thing," but their "hearts never changed." Even the laws of the Old Testament in the Bible only revealed man's sin nature and his need for a savior. It was Jesus Christ that paid the price for Adam's rebellion and our sin nature, restoring us back to our original place with God (only when we choose to accept Him and his finished work as our Savior, and allow Him to be the Lord of our lives).

It was then that I understood what God meant in 2012 when He said to me, "It cannot be accomplished by the marches of the 1960's, but by a spiritual revolution." Only when men and women have a true encounter with the real person of Jesus Christ can change occur. A true relationship with Jesus Christ, not just knowing about God, tradition, or religion. Man is unable to save himself.

My starting point was to admit that I had a problem. My problem was that I could not understand how a just God could allow such injustice to last so long without holding people accountable for their actions. Yes, I had a problem! I wanted them to reap what they had sown and pay for the pain that they had caused so many innocent people for no other reason than they were born with darker skin. In my little mind, a person had no right to determine another human being's worth. While I knew that I loved God and was saved, I found that I had much more to learn. I would never be able to truly experience my inheritance in Jesus Christ, nor would our nation experience a spiritual revolution, until God's people admitted that a problem existed, even in the house of God.

Only when true believers are willing to relinquish their right to be white, black, or yellow—and accept their true identity as children of God—will God be invited to help us do something about racism. I wanted to experience the manifestation of being truly free and whole, independent of the circumstances in this world. Once I acknowledged my problem, I needed to expose the trick of the enemy among other believers who, either out of ignorance of God's word or selfish pride, had allowed this evil force to fester in their hearts for generations. I knew that according to God's word, the change had to start in us (the believer). No need to point fingers at the world when we behave worse than they do. We are the ones that claim to know God. It was the mixed signals of believers that forced me to delve into God's word for answers. What I have found is fascinating and was the beginning of my own personal healing.

Research into God's original plan for mankind, how that plan applies to our nation and my life, and how this plan can positively impact our world and the hearts of men was my starting point. Using God's word and carefully using the history of the United States, I explore the African American experience from one Christian African American female's perspective. Just as an inventor provides instructions on how to best use his product, so has the creator given us guidelines for how to best live this life. The word of God is also God's last will and testament to us, a covenant between God and his people. It tells us our inheritance, our identity, and our authority, but it also tells us what happens when we violate and disobey his word. As an African American woman, this has been the only positive source for my identity. The world's view of me had left me damaged and scarred, only because I believed the lie of another human being influenced by satan, rather than believing the words of my Creator.

I consider myself simply a messenger with a message, under the authority of God. Therefore, it is not my intention to condemn, blame, or accuse anyone. Likewise, it is not my responsibility to convince, debate, or defend that which can only be done by the Spirit of God. Since God (in his sovereignty) chose to give us "freedom of choice," the option given us to choose to hear and obey God remains a part of God's covenant of love. I pray that every reader will approach this read with an open heart, even as I have made every attempt to open myself only to the Spirit of God, despite my feelings, opinions, and experiences. It is my intention to research both the natural and spiritual aspects of the issue of racism. This has been no easy journey, but it was worth revisiting painful experiences in order to find the truth and begin the process of healing.

SECTION 1

A Life Worth Living

The Face in the Mirror

The face in the mirror peered back at me. I could see the worry lines and sad eyes that had formed over the years from allowing the cares of the world to weigh heavy on my heart. Deep down inside, I knew that there was more to me than met the eye. I knew that in the eyes of the world, I was an African American female in her early sixties with very little value and worth. It seemed that many of our black men had even begun to agree with the world's view of me. They were not privileged to see the inside of my heart, for if they had seen it, they probably would have not been so quick to judge. After all, this outer skin is not the real me.

It had been fifty-six years since I first became acquainted with the love of my life. Now, at age sixty-two, I was fighting for my life and struggling to remain committed to a love that my natural senses told me had failed me. It amazed me that despite the disappointments, unfulfilled dreams, and unkept promises, deep down inside me, *He* was still the love of my life.

I couldn't explain it. Life certainly had not turned out as I had believed it would when I was first introduced to him at six years old, some fifty-six years ago. To think that He loved me just like I was made an instant impression on my innocent little mind. You see, I was a normal six-year-old with all the excitement, optimism, and confidence that children have before they are tainted by the world's view. If I had only continued to listen to what the word of God said about me instead of the world's opinion of me, I probably would not have encountered the frustrations that I met over the next few decades. Instead, I listened to what I heard, saw, and felt, only to find myself in the fight for my life.

Being born in the South as an African American in 1955 was not a reason to rejoice. Yet it took me ten years to find out that the world's view of me was quite different from *His* view of me. Why had I listened to them instead of *Him*? I understood why I had trouble accepting his love, since my world reflected everything except love. To my life's credit, I had a failed marriage, years of useless degrees, a career that failed to bless the very people that I was called to bless, and two wonderful sons whose hopes and dreams dissipated before my very eyes.

At the age of ten, I realized that my ancestors had a very different experience in America than most Americans. My little mind had trouble seeing "love" in that experience. My optimism of "being loved" began to crumble at that point and continued to suffer until this day. It was when I went back to my first love for answers that I began to understand what was behind everything that had happened to me in life.

It seems that God meets us at the point of our need, and I needed the truth now more than ever before—the whole truth and nothing but the truth. An alternate truth would not do; the truth that comes only from the one who created me was the only answer. It was this desperation for truth that led me to search both the Word of God and the history of our nation for answers. I turned to the only true source that I knew: the mirror of God's word. I had to constantly remind myself that the words of King David to God about himself, also applied to me: "I will praise thee; for I am fearfully *and* wonderfully made: marvellous *are* thy works; and *that* my soul knoweth right well" (Psalm 139:14, KJV). So although the world's system had devalued me, God had said that I was amazingly and miraculously made (by Him). If anyone knew me, the Creator certainly did.

When I think about the physical body and all of its systems, organs, muscles, tissues, cells, joints, etc. all working together as one complex system, I can honestly praise Almighty God. The intricacies of the body alone are a constant reminder to me of the majesty of God. Only God could make something so phenomenal as the human body. Whether white, black, or yellow, the body has all of the same organs, systems, tissues, joints, muscles, etc. Only the color of the skin separates us; even our blood is the same color (red). Yet skin color (exterior organ) has been a form of division my entire life—and long before I was conceived in my mother's womb. I do know that division and confusion are not from God; it is not his character. The question then is, who and/or what is responsible for this division?

> But even if our gospel is [in some sense] hidden [behind a veil], it is hidden [only] to those who are perishing; among them *the god of this world [satan]* has blinded the minds of the unbeliev-ing to prevent them from seeing the illuminating light of the gospel of the glory of Christ, who is the image of God. (1 Corinthians 4:3–4, AMP)

The god of this world (satan) is responsible for influencing men and women of all nations, race, etc. It was when I listened to a series on *Breaking Controlling Spirits* (the Leviathan spirit) by Dr. Lance Wallnau that I began to understand why the racial divide is preva-lent in our nation and in the Body of Christ. Unfortunately, decep-tion and twisting words/appearances to mean something they were not intended remain satan's greatest weapon. He uses deception to divide people along racial, denominational, political, and even doc-trinal lines. While we fight one another, he advances his kingdom of darkness. Hosea 4:6 says, "*My people* are destroyed from lack of knowledge. Because you have rejected knowledge, I also reject you as my priests; because you have ignored the *law of your God*, I also will ignore your children" (AMP).

The face that I saw in the mirror is only one part of me (my body). However, I learned that the human was made in the image and likeness of our Father God. In the beginning, we were created with God's nature (love, truth, etc.), and we were given dominion over the earth. But man's disobedience caused us to lose God's nature and take on a sin nature (the nature of satan). We also lost dominion over the earth, and satan legally gained this dominion from us after the fall of man.

> Now may the God of peace Himself sanctify you
> through and through [that is, separate you from
> profane and vulgar things, make you pure and
> whole and undamaged—consecrated to Him—
> set apart for His purpose]; and may your spirit
> and soul and body be kept complete and [be
> found] blameless at the coming of our Lord Jesus
> Christ. (1 Thessalonians 5:23, AMP)

It was interesting to know that God is a Spirit, and so are we, because we were created in his image and likeness. "God is spirit [the Source of life, yet invisible to mankind], and those who worship Him must worship in spirit and truth" (John 4:24, AMP). God's nature is *love*, He *is love*, and so is the person born again.

> Beloved, let us [unselfishly] love *and* seek the best
> for one another, for love is from God; and every-
> one who loves [others] is born of God and knows
> God [through personal experience]. The one
> who does not love has not become acquainted
> with God [does not and never did know Him],
> for God is love. [He is the originator of love, and
> it is an enduring attribute of His nature.] (1 John
> 4:7–8, AMP).

> And hope maketh not ashamed; because the *love
> of God is shed* abroad *in our hearts by the Holy
> Ghost* which is given unto us. (Romans 5:5,
> AMP)

If we are made in the image of God, we need to know more about God and mankind and God's original plan for mankind. God is three distinct persons, each of whom is God, all operating as one person.

1. *God the Father* is the Creator of heaven and earth. His kingdom is heaven; however, when He created mankind, He gave him dominion of the earth (because He loved us). This dominion was not to rule over another man, but instead, as Genesis 1:26 says, "And God said, Let *us* make *man in our image, after our likeness*: and *let them have dominion* over the fish of the sea, and over the fowl of the air, and over the cattle, and over all the earth, and over every creeping thing that creepeth upon the earth."

   - Because of God's love, He also gave man freedom to choose what he would do, say, and believe.
   - Adam (the first man) represented the human race and chose to disobey God's instructions about eating from the tree of the knowledge of good and evil. This choice caused Adam to die spiritually (take on satan's nature, become separated from God, and lose his dominion of the earth).
   - Just as the president of the United States makes decisions that impacts all of its citizens, Adam's decision impacted all mankind from the time of his disobedience until now—man is born into a fallen world.

2. *God the Son* (Jesus [Son of Man], Christ [Son of God]) is the Word of God. Jesus speaks to perform the will of God. Throughout creation, we constantly see the words "And God said."

   - In an effort to restore us back to God, after the fall of mankind, God sent his Son, the Word of God, to earth. He became a substitute for the sin of mankind.
   - John 1:1, 14 says, "In the beginning [before all time] was the Word (Christ), and the Word was with God, and the Word was God Himself. And the Word (Christ) became flesh, and lived among us; and we [actually] saw His glory, glory as belongs to the [One

and] only begotten *Son* of the Father, [the Son who is truly unique, the only One of His kind, who is] full of grace and truth (absolutely free of deception)."

3. *God's Spirit* (the Spirit of God, the Holy Spirit) makes God's word come alive in us, as we yield our spirit to the Holy Spirit of God.

Mankind is a three-part being, just as God is three persons. First Thessalonians 5:23 notes, "Now may the God of peace Himself sanctify you through and through [that is, separate you from profane and vulgar things, make you pure and whole and undamaged—consecrated to Him—set apart for His purpose]; and *may your spirit and soul and body* be kept complete and [be found] blameless at the coming of our Lord Jesus Christ."

1. *Human Spirit* is the real man (hidden man of the heart). It is only this part of man that is recreated at the new birth, when we are born again (accept Jesus as our Savior). Although we take on a new nature (God's nature), we still must choose to submit our spirit to the Holy Spirit (Spirit of God) and trust the grace of God to daily keep us. Keep in mind that in the beginning, God blew into man's nostrils the breath of life, so our true nature should be like God. It was the fall of man (his disobedience) that caused us to take on satan's nature.

2. *Soul of man* consists of the *mind, the will, and the emotions.* Although we may be born again, our soul and body did not get saved. We are responsible for our soul and body.

   Therefore I urge you, brothers and sisters, by the mercies of God, to *present your bodies* [dedicating all of yourselves, set apart] as a living sacrifice, holy and well-pleasing to God, *which is* your rational (logical, intelligent) act of worship. And do not be conformed to this world [any longer with its superficial values and customs], but *be transformed and* progressively changed [as you mature spiritually] *by the renewing of your mind* [focusing on godly values and ethical attitudes], so that you may prove [for yourselves] what the will of God is, that which is good and acceptable and perfect [in His plan and purpose for you]. (Romans 12:1–2, AMP)

So get rid of all uncleanness and all that remains of wickedness, and with a humble spirit *receive the word* [of God] which is implanted [actually rooted in *your* heart], *which is able to save your souls.* (James 1:21)

3. *Body of man,* including the skin is the part of mankind that is needed to exist on the earth. No one can see our spirit or our soul, but they see the exterior of the person, which may have a black, white, brown, or yellowish complexion. However, that it not the real person.

Andrew Womack said in an article on Spirit, Soul, and Body, "We are spirit beings, the ultimate way to control bad behavior isn't by more laws, metal detectors, or social engineering, it's changing the hearts of people, one at a time. Only Jesus can do that." Only when we yield our human spirits to the spirit of God will we see change among the people of God. Paul called immature Christians carnal minded. We become a new creation in our spirit when we are born again; however, we must choose to renew our mind with the Word of God, present our bodies as living sacrifices to God, and our mouth must align itself with God's word and not the latest trend, tradition, or religion.

The Call

"Except you love all my people, you cannot minister to any of my people." These were the words that I heard in 1986 as I sought God in preparation to minister in music at a visiting church in Petersburg, Virginia. I had always loved God's people (*all of them*). However, my experiences had left me hating the behavior of anyone who felt themselves superior to me or any other human being.

"Feed my sheep," I had heard within me. What exactly did this mean? At that time, I had no idea that these were the words that Jesus had said to Peter in response to Peter's claim that he loved Jesus (John 21:15–17, KJV). Little did I know that this would be the first time God would allow me to minister to an all-Caucasian congregation.

Race really should not have mattered, but it did. Experiences from my past had left me suspicious of all things Caucasian (even among "believers"). I had been invited by an African American sergeant in the army, who was a pastor, but also worked in the same government agency as I had. He was affiliated with this church and had agreed to find a visiting soloist for their revival. Unfortunately, I had automatically assumed that if he was African American, the congregation would be African American also.

As I fumbled to find the address to the church, I finally parked in a lot overflowing with cars. Obviously, I was late, and service had already begun. As I helped my eight-year-old and three-year-old sons from the car, I entered the sanctuary and noticed that there was not one African American in the house (not even the sergeant that had invited me). Immediately, I backed out of the door and hurriedly headed back to my car, carrying one son and guiding the other. With no GPS or Google Maps to guide me, I proceeded to back out of the lot, assuming I was at the wrong church. My eight-year-old asked me a profound question that forced me to take a good look at myself and search my own heart. "Why did we leave, mom", he asked.

"We must be at the wrong church," I replied.

"Why", he asked. Inside me, I heard the words, "Yes, why?"

Recently divorced, the lack of security and protection had resurfaced from my childhood. Turning the car around, I headed back to the church and parked the car. As I entered the foyer of the church again, I whispered a prayer to God for protection for me and my sons and proceeded to enter the sanctuary.

Apparently knowing my apprehension, the minister in the pulpit announced that the guest soloist had arrived, and he immediately invited me and my sons to come forward. Seating my sons on the front seat with the deacons, I proceeded to the pulpit to sing the songs that I felt God had laid on my heart for this body of believers.

As I sang the first song ("Jesus, We Give You the Glory"), my eyes fell on a young lady in the audience with three toddlers on her side and an infant in her arms. As she wept vehemently, the words that I had heard in my private prayer time with God came back to my mind: "Except you love all my people, you cannot minister to any of my people." My heart melted as I watched her tears flowing. I wasn't sure if she was hurting personally, or if she understood my reason for distrust. Fear left me, and I understood what God had meant. It was at that point that I realized that I needed to be healed from the wounds that I had buried deep down inside me for many decades. I had to be whole in order for me to share healing and the love of God to all people. All I know was that night, God started me on a journey that has taken many twists and turns. I believe that his ultimate desire was to heal me and bring me to wholeness so that I could better reflect Jesus in every area of my life.

Many years had passed since that Friday in 1986 when God had told me to love all his people. Yet I continued to seek healing for myself so that I could be a blessing to others. I honestly believed that I loved all God's people, although I didn't understand God's love for me. Somehow, slavery and the impact of racism did not reflect Gods love for me. We all have challenges in life, but my challenge had always been finding the love of God in slavery, racism, injustice, and oppression. Knowing that "Christians" had promoted slavery had left me wondering about Christianity. Although I had been told that God was a white man's god, I knew that this was a lie from hell. So I had to find what was missing from my life, knowing that failure is never God.

Despite these plaguing questions, I continued to seek God for answers. There was a hole in my heart, which I had tried to fill unsuccessfully. I spent every waking moment trying to understand the truth of God's word and my conflicting reality. Watching my two sons struggle with believing God's love for them forced me to inquire of God again. This time the words came back: *It cannot be accomplished by the marches of the 1960s, but by a spiritual revolution.*

I had my thoughts about what God meant by a spiritual revolution, but wanted to know what God's thoughts were on this matter. God's words to me in 1986, "Feed my sheep," now meant more to me than anything else. I wanted to obey God, but felt I had nothing to feed the people. I knew about God, but needed to "know God and be known of God." What was the "good news" for African Americans?

I had loved God all my life and had made every attempt to live for Him privately and publicly. However, now I was struggling with my own faith. I needed to know why oppression had lasted generation after generation. How could people who claim to love God hate me only because of the color of my skin (for which I had no control)? Loving all his people did not mean loving certain groups of people, but it meant to love all people groups. Should they not be required to love me also? Again, I knew God allows us to choose to hear and obey Him. He would not force me nor them to follow his way of doing things. We had to choose to yield our will to his will and his way. That's just the kind of God He is. He could force us, but his nature is love. Love does not force itself on another.

Desperate to understand God's ways after my encounter in 1986, I had started ministry school in 1991 in Oklahoma for the sole purpose of seeking God through His word. I had to have an answer. However, I had only completed one of two years of ministry school and returned to Birmingham where I went back into the classroom. Now, after twenty-one years in the classroom, I had come to realize that as much as I wanted to be a blessing to my students, I was grieved when I looked into the hopeless eyes of my sons, students, and others that I passed by in life. I wanted to assure them that everything would be fine, but I had begun to question God's faithfulness to me and all his people (especially people of color). What was the good news? Who would believe me if I told them the good news when they looked at the outcome of my life? Should I settle for less than the promises of God because I was darker?

I was determined to hear from God alone. I could not afford to hear additional opinions of men. It had to be the truth, and only God could grant me that truth. In 2013, I decided to retire and return to ministry school to give total focus to God and complete ministry training that I had started in 1991 in Oklahoma. I wondered if the reason for my emptiness and inability to bless others might be because I had avoided the call into the ministry. Now, I was willing to totally surrender. I had to truly know God, so that I would no longer continue explaining away what was happening in life to certain groups of people.

Excited to be among other believers being trained for the ministry, I expected to spend the next two years in the Word of God and basking in the presence of God. Instead, I came as close to hell as I had come on earth. The only purpose of the many attacks was to distract me and move my focus from God so that I would not fulfill God's plan. Satan's main purpose was to silence my voice.

Silence the Voice

As I delve into the Word of God, the reflection that I saw of my life was very disturbing. I had spent over thirty years in the classroom pouring myself into young lives, hoping to make a difference in their lives. Although I sought God (the Master Teacher) for directions on how to be a blessing to my students and those that I worked with and worked for, I seemed to be the enemy to those that I wanted so desperately to bless.

Waiting to remarry the only man that had ever touched me, thirty years later I realized that even though I had repented for divorcing and had desired to do things God's way, God would not violate someone else's choice. I had two wonderful sons, but had ignorantly trained them as an Old Testament believer (under the Law, the Ten Commandments), instead of teaching them to accept the grace of God through Jesus and his finished works. With no way of working or performing enough to be successful, I and my sons remained frustrated with life and never able to measure up to the world's view of success.

These and other realizations sent me back to reexamine myself and my life. I knew that the way of a transgressor is hard (Proverbs 13:15, KJV), and since life had been far from easy, I wondered how I had transgressed. Not understanding grace, I sought to understand where I had missed God. I heard in my spirit, "Finish what you started." As I pondered those words, there were only three things I recalled that I had not completed in life: my marriage, a master's degree at Howard University, and ministry school.

After thirty years of waiting to remarry, I had decided to repent for divorce and move on with my life. I knew that God hated divorce, and so did I. However, God still honored freedom of choice, and since God loved my husband as much as God loved me, God would not force him to love me. So, I decided to release him and move on with my life.

It was too late to continue the master of science degree at Howard University because seven years had elapsed since I began the degree in Computer Science.

The only thing remaining that I had not completed was ministry school. Since in 1986 I had heard in prayer, "Feed my sheep," I automatically assumed that I had been called into ministry. However, at the time I didn't believe in women ministers, so I had failed to complete the training in 1991. I immediately began to assume that finishing Bible Training College was the meaning of "Finish What You Started."

With a desperate desire for an answer from God and a determination to change the trajectory of my life, in 2013 I decided to retire from my teaching job and relocate to Oklahoma to finish ministry college, believing I would finally be in the will of God, and everything in life would change for the better. Little did I know that I would become acquainted with Paul's thorn in the flesh, messengers from satan (2 Corinthians 12:7).

My traumatic experience began with believers, not people in the world. Instead of spending two years in the presence of God, I felt as if I had entered hell on earth (a complete description of this experience can be found in my novel *Struggle Without: Struggle Within*). Satan influenced God's people to slander my name, harass me, and defame my character in Oklahoma, and influenced people to follow me back to my hometown, continuing slanderous accusations. It was then that I realized that these slanderous accusations were meant to be distractions in an attempt to silence my voice on something that had plagued me and our nation from our nation's inception.

Without intending to, I had become obsessed with correcting whatever problem existed that had my life spiraling into defeat. Excited about the possible outcome of learning how to be obedient to God, nothing would keep me from fulfilling God's purpose for my life.

I honestly had expected to spend three years in God's word, basking in God's presence, among believers called into the ministry just like myself. I simply wanted to know my God, know that He truly loved me, and ensure that the world knew that this African American woman belonged to God and was loved by God. "*Saying*, Touch not mine anointed, and do my prophets no harm" (1 Chronicles 16:22, Psalm 105:15; KJV).

Unfortunately, life had another plan. While the study of God's word was powerful and exciting, I felt even more betrayed by God. Not only had I left everything and everyone, but I had purposefully attempted to pull away, be alone with God, and learn of Him. I had always known that God sees everything, even when people don't see, so I had purposed to glorify God in my public and private life. Now, as lies were spread by people that I should have been able to trust, without God vindicating me, the feeling of betrayal only grew stronger. What do you do when you know you've done all you know to do and still nothing goes right? Knowing that I had to assume responsibility for the outcome of my life didn't soften the blow because I had done all I knew to do.

After graduation from Bible Training College, I was so ready to return home; yet God was not finished with me. Though He constantly reminded me, "I'll never leave you or forsake you," He seemed so far away; yet I knew that I had to remain faithful and obey God.

After another year of ministry school, I graduated from the School of Biblical Studies and was released by God to return home to Alabama. If I had thought the nightmare was over, I was sadly mistaken. Upon my arrival back in Birmingham, I was constantly trailed and harassed by men and women (mostly white). Prior to Oklahoma, I had never experienced such harassment. I had never been so disrespected and dishonored before arriving in Oklahoma. Before my experience in Oklahoma, I thought this type of thing happened only in the movies, and only to important people, not to ordinary people who are just trying to love God and live life according to his word.

I had to learn to trust God again. From childhood, my trust in the system and mankind had been damaged, but I had always trusted God. He had been the only one that I could trust. Now I felt like my trust in everyone and everything had been destroyed. Then I remembered what God's word said about it: "For we wrestle not against flesh and blood, but against principalities, against powers, against the rulers of the darkness of this world, against spiritual wickedness in high *places*" (Ephesians 6:12).

Though I had been trailed to my home, church, hospitals, neighborhoods, and even the nursing home, I finally realized that these people (some claimed to be Christians) were influenced by satan. The aloneness that I had felt for more than three years had left me more unsure of God's love for me than ever. After all, the systems of this world had obviously not been established for my good. I had been brave all these years, though alone, because I sincerely believed that God would protect me. However, this experience seemed to destroy my faith; yet God continued to unfold what had happened and the reason behind it.

Fear had turned into anger because of what satan had done and how he used God's people to begin slandering and defaming my character. I was tired of believing God and feeling defeated by evil men. I had made a last-ditch effort to obey God, expecting the favor of God, but instead feeling totally betrayed by God.

I knew that God was my protector, but his work is accomplished through people on earth. In the past, at least I had the hope that black men valued me as a person; but now, even they seemed to no longer value me. Not all white nor all black men are the problem, yet there seem to be no one that I could trust. I was struggling to continue committing to someone who appeared to demonstrate that I was not as important to Him as the white race. God had been my only hope, and now that hope was slowly drifting away. Then I found these words in his word: "Hope deferred maketh the heart sick: but *when* the desire cometh, *it is* a tree of life" (Proverbs 13:12).

> I will praise thee; for I am fearfully *and* wonder-
> fully made: marvellous *are* thy works; and *that*
> my soul knoweth right well. (Psalms 139:14)

I continued to seek God for answers. Each Sunday, I saw the exhortation, "The Word of God is the Answer". It was this word of exhortation from my Pastor and other men and women of God that kept me focused and determined to truly know God. I knew that satan's use of people as his messengers to destroy me, my credibility, and those that I love was his method to distract me. He is known for coming to steal, kill and destroy anyone who will allow him.

Silencing my voice from experiencing and proclaiming the "Good News" of redemption was his plan. Although I always knew that he was behind these attacks, it took me a while to understand his purpose. I asked God to give me the grace to focus on God rather than on my circumstances. I had to choose to trust and believe God again, because everything in my circumstances said He was not trustworthy for me. As I decided to believe again; I noticed that God began to reveal more of Himself to me. He gave me more grace to deal with the taunts from people who unknowingly were being influenced and used by satan.

I was determined to know the truth about God and his relationship to me and people who look like me. The strongholds in this area had been a part of my race since this nation was formed, and satan was not about to release it without a fight. Yet I knew that I had to continue to pursue the truth. After all, if I couldn't trust God, I was already dead.

A Life Worth Living

Although I had always loved God, lived every waking moment of my life trying to please Him, nothing had worked out for me. Things looked fine on the outside, but inside was a raging storm. That's why this manuscript was so difficult. As I looked back over my life, I was very dissatisfied with the results of living a Christian life. I had always had a problem with the station of African Americans in the United States, especially African American Christians. I wondered about the blood of Jesus, *Was there a different blood shed for African Americans than others on the cross?* When God said that he loved the world and He gave his only Son, were African Americans not a part of the world He was referring to?

I had believed that being a Christian set me apart from the world, not because I was better than they, but because of what the word said about my new-found relationship with Jesus and the benefits that it brought. Perhaps I misunderstood what the Bible meant, but something definitely was wrong.

When she was alive, my mom always told me that when something went wrong in life, "the failure was not in God." While I appreciated this reminder, I couldn't help but wonder how this knowledge could help me live this life. Since I had done all that I knew to do to live a life pleasing to God, I wondered how I could witness for Jesus when the world looked and mocked me for my belief, which didn't seem to be working for me. How could I explain to my sons about God's goodness when they looked upon me with horror as they, too, looked at the world in which we lived compared to what the word said about our lives? I knew that the Word had said, "Many are the afflictions of the righteous;" however, it continued to say that (Psalms 34:19; KJV) "the Lord delivered them from them all."

While I claimed being more than a conqueror—always triumphant, head and not the tail, above only and not beneath—many times, I felt anything but victorious. How could I balance this truth (God's word) with the reality of my life (satanic contradictions)? I didn't expect everything in life to be a bed or roses, but God had said He would cause all things to work out for my good (Romans 8:28).

The amazing thing about all of this was I still loved God more than anything in this world. Although nothing had worked out for me, there was something on the inside that wanted to dig into the Word to find out why things were not working. Yes, I had my time of blaming God, feeling betrayed by God, wallowing in self-pity, and wanting to give up; however, I had no desire to face this life without knowing Almighty God. Even if God gave me everything that I thought I desired, the thought of not pleasing Him, not having a close and intimate relationship with Him, sent chills through me. God was the only reason that I would want to exist on the earth.

To understand how an African American Christian woman could live a fulfilled life on earth led me to go back to the beginning of creation. The beginning spiritually and naturally (i.e., from the word of God and from the history of the United States of America). As I sought God on why racism was still as ugly as when I was a little girl, I begin to understand what God had meant when He said, "It cannot be accomplished by the marches of the 1960s, but by a spiritual revolution."

I know that the marches of the 1960s had men and women who were led by the Spirit of God; however, forming laws without the hearts of men changing was not the solution to the problem of racism. Douglas MacArthur stated that rules are mostly made to be broken and are too often for the lazy to hide behind (1962). I believe that the Word of God (Holy Bible) is the answer to every problem that we encounter in life. Despite degrees, monies, and positions in society, only God can give us an answer to what is happening in our world today. While the focus of this book is on the USA and racism, this message could apply to any country in the world, any problem, and any people.

"It cannot be accomplished by the marches of the 1960s, but by a spiritual revolution."

These were the words that welled up within me as I sought God about race relations in the United States late one summer day in 2012. I had wondered since age ten in 1965 until 2017 how the truth of God's word and my reality in life were so different. As an African American *Christian* woman, the wounds were so deep that it took five years from that day in 2012 to be able to get the right words from my heart to the pages of this book. I knew that regardless to my feelings, the only truth was God's word. Only his word would set me and others free. God's word, from his heart, (not based upon my convenience, my interpretation, or my opinion). This meant that I had to spend time alone with the Lord, in his presence to get his perspective, and to avoid any biases that I might have. The purpose of this book deals with how we began and continue to struggle with the same issues of yesterday.

Knowing in my heart that the only way to get a solution to any problem was to seek God, I had been in prayer about this matter for several years. I believed in my heart that there was nothing too hard for God (Jehovah), yet after more than fifty years of believing and seeing unchanged hearts, I was in the fight for my life and my faith. If I could only find out how we got to this point historically, find out what God says about our condition, and determine what actions God says must be taken to reach a solution.

Since the Gospel is supposed to be "Good News" for all people, and God has given the believer the ministry of reconciliation, my goal is to expose darkness, reveal truth, and allow God to show us his answer to the problem of racism. In the process of seeking God's perspective, his healing power had to flow through me, in me, and from me, affecting others who would in turn influence their world, and eventually bring healing to our land. It seems that it would be an obvious solution; however, after combatting racism for over fifty years, I needed an answer that only God could provide. Although racism is a symptom of a deeper spiritual problem, it has impacted my life more than anything else. Therefore, I wanted a clear understanding of what racism is.

Racism is defined as

> a belief that race is the primary determinant of human traits and capacities and that racial differences produce an inherent superiority of a particular race, a doctrine or political program based on the assumption of racism and designed to execute its principles, a political or social system founded on racism, or racial prejudice or discrimination.[1]

"If a man says, I love God, and hateth his brother, he is a liar: for he that loveth not his brother whom he hath seen, how can he love God whom he hath not seen? And this commandment have we from him, That he who loveth God love his brother also" (1 John 4:20–21).

The verses above were written by John to emphasize the life of a true child of God. No matter how I tried to see the love of God, my current world showed a different picture. Nevertheless, being a child of God before being African American, I remembered that just as God (through Jesus Christ) reconciled the world to Himself, He expected believers (including me) to handle things differently.

> Therefore, if anyone is in Christ, the new creation has come: The old has gone, the new is here! All this is from God, who reconciled us to himself through Christ and gave us the ministry of reconciliation: that God was reconciling the world to himself in Christ, not counting people's sins against them. And he has committed to us the message of reconciliation. (2 Corinthians 5:17–19, NIV)

This did not mean we were to pretend there was no problem. Instead, we were to seek God's perspective on the situation and han-

---

[1.] "Racism." Merriam-Webster.com. https://www.merriam-webster.com/racism.

dle it as He would. I had to be very careful with God's word. I realized that many people were skeptical of God's word because it had been used to manipulate and oppress people in the past. Instead of spending enough time in God's word and in his presence, people used God's word incorrectly to justify their evil hearts instead of rightly dividing God's word. I now had to be careful that I didn't become so set on my opinion that my opinion was more important to me than the Word of God and the Spirit behind his word.

As much as I wanted to blame others for the outcome of my life, the more I studied God's word, the more I realized that in God I had unlimited potential, possibilities, and protection. The key was to know how to apply his word to my life in a way that his word would impact my life more than my circumstances. I had to delve deep into our natural history and use the mirror of God's word to understand the world in which I live. This study was imperative because I knew if I had silently struggled more than fifty years, there might be someone else silently dying inside. It grieved me to think there might be someone unable to experience the love of God because I and other believers had failed to submit to God and allow his Holy Spirit to purify our hearts as we renew our minds with his word. We cannot imitate one we do not know. Many believers "know about" our Savior, but they may not truly know Him. Paul the apostle prayed this prayer for the believer:

> I keep asking that the God of our Lord Jesus Christ, the glorious Father, *may give you the Spirit of wisdom and revelation, so that you may know him better.* I pray that the eyes of your heart may be enlightened in order that you may know the hope to which he has called you, the riches of his glorious inheritance in his holy people, and his incomparably great power for us who believe. That power is the same as the mighty strength he exerted when he raised Christ from the dead and seated him at his right hand in the heavenly realms, far above all rule and authority, power

and dominion, and every name that is invoked, not only in the present age but also in the one to come. And God placed all things under his feet and appointed him to be head over everything for the church, which is his body, the fullness of him who fills everything in every way. (Ephesians 1:17–23)

SECTION 2

God and Mankind

It Was All Good

To better understand myself and my circumstances, I had to understand my beginnings. Just as any creation, only the creator knows the intricacies of his creation. Just as an inventor gives us an instruction manual for how his product works, and how to effectively use the product, so too has God given us his word to be used (not only as an instruction manual on how to live a successful life [Joshua 1:8], but also as a last will and testament to tell us who we are, what we have, and what we can do in this life [not just when we get to heaven]). So as any good student, I turned to the source (God's word) to determine the truth about myself and to answer the plaguing questions about my life and existence. In studying, I found that it is not God's character to force anyone to do anything. We must choose to do what God instructs us to do.

My first step was to repent for not making God's word priority in my life. Psalm 139:4 says, "Even before a word is on my tongue, behold, O Lord, you know it altogether." It is a slap in the face of God to take the opinion of another human being about who I am over the description of me by the Creator Himself. I began to understand why things are the way that they are.

Since we are created in the image of God after his likeness, it is important that we know how that image looks. I began to investigate the character of God, just so I could know what I should be like. I had to know in my heart that He was in fact the God for *all* who accepted Him, regardless of race or experiences in life. What I found really excited me as I began to better understand what was happening in our world.

You see, it was not always this way, with hatred, selfishness, and evil. It was never intended for man to suffer and be so self-centered.

In Genesis 1–2, it shows that God created the heavens, the earth, and everything in it—including mankind (Adam and Eve). Everything God created in the beginning was good. Look at God's creation from his word, and you will see what is happening in our world today.

In the Beginning

In the beginning God (*Elohim*) created [by forming
from nothing] the heavens and the earth.

—Genesis 1:1 (AMP)

Then God said, "*Let us (Father, Son, Holy Spirit) make man in
Our image, according to Our likeness* [not physical, but a spiritual
personality and more likeness]; *and let them have complete authority*
over the fish of the sea, the birds of the air, the cattle, and over
the entire earth, and over everything that creeps and crawls on
the earth." So *God created man in His own image, in the image and
likeness of God He created him; male and female created He them.*

—Genesis 1:26–27 (AMP)

God saw *everything that He had made*, and behold, it
was *very good and* He validated it completely. And there
was evening and there was morning, a sixth day.

—Genesis 1:31 (AMP)

Then the LORD *God formed* [that is, created the body
of] *man from the dust of the ground*, and *breathed into
his nostrils the breath of life*; and the man became a living
being [an individual complete in body and spirit].

—Genesis 2:7, (AMP)

So, the LORD GOD CAUSED A DEEP SLEEP TO FALL UPON ADAM; AND WHILE HE SLEPT, HE TOOK ONE OF HIS RIBS AND closed up the flesh at that place. And the rib which the LORD GOD HAD TAKEN FROM THE MAN HE MADE (FASHIONED, FORMED) INTO A WOMAN, AND HE BROUGHT HER *and* presented her to the man.

—Genesis 2:21–22 (AMP)

As I peered into the Bible and read the words about God's original creation, my heart leaped for joy. What had happened from the time that God said that everything that He had made was very good until 2017 when racism was higher than it had been since the civil rights era? When we look at God as Creator, the passage shows several things:

1. God created the heavens and the earth and everything that is in the earth.
2. God made mankind (male and female) *in his image*. Notice that the verse says in *our* image, after *our* likeness. Our image suggests more than one. God Himself is a triune being, one God with three distinct personalities. God the Father is the Creator, the Word of God (God the Son, in the person of Jesus Christ), and the Spirit of God (God the Holy Spirit).
3. God gave mankind dominion over fish of the sea, fowl of the air, cattle, and over all the earth and every creeping thing on the earth.
4. Everything that God made was very good.

As I read through the creation in Genesis 1 and 2, I noticed that God *made* man (mankind) in Genesis 1:26–27, and God *formed* man in Genesis 2:7. It was fascinating to know that *God is a Spirit*, and therefore, in Genesis 1, God created mankind as a spirit being. Human beings (mankind, male and female), had the divine nature of God at creation. Notice that, in Genesis 1:26, *God said*, "Let *us* make man in *our* image, after *our* likeness." Mankind's spirit was spoken into existence by the Word of God (Jesus; John 1:1, 14).

However, in Genesis 2:7, man's body was formed from the dust of the earth. Although male and female both originally had the divine nature of God in their spirit, man's body came about by the Father God molding the dust of the ground and giving man his breath (the breath of God, the breath of life). It wasn't until Genesis 2:21 that the woman was formed. Woman was not formed out of one of man's many ribs, of which he would not feel the loss. She is one side of man; and though he may have several sides to his nature and character, yet without woman, one integral portion of him is wanting.[2]

The text above tells me that *mankind (human race, male and female) were originally created in the image and likeness of the Godhead.* This meant that man had the nature of God in his spirit when originally created. The first man created became the federal head for the entire human race. Just as the president of the United States represents the citizens of the United States, and the decisions made by the president impacts all the citizens, it was the same with Adam in representing mankind. We were to be like God. The way God handled things was the way we were to handle things. God created the universe with his words ("and God said"). God blessed mankind and gave him dominion (authority) of the earth realm (irrespective of race or gender).

> "All authority (all power of absolute rule) in heaven and on earth has been given to Me. Go therefore and make disciples of all the nations[help the people to learn of Me, believe in Me, and obey My words], baptizing them in the name of the *Father and of the Son and of the Holy Spirit,* teaching them to observe everything that I have commanded you; and lo, I am with you always [remaining with you perpetually—regard-

---

[2] "Ellicott's Commentary for English Readers," Bible Hub, http://biblehub.com/commentaries/ellicott/genesis/2.htm.

less of circumstance, and on every occasion],
even to the end of the age." (Matthew 28:18–20)

He even planted a garden to provide for man's food. God gave instructions for replenishing the earth, what food to eat, and what man needed to do to live a fulfilling life. Being a God of love, He did not take away man's choice. *Man had the choice to obey God or disobey God.* God's love is not forceful. He presents his word as a guide, but ultimately, He gives us the right to choose to obey or disobey. It must be understood that just as there are consequences for obedience, there are also consequences for disobedience.

To better understand myself, I had to understand the Godhead (since we are created in the image and likeness of Him). The remaining chapters in this section explain who God is (as Father, as Son, and as Holy Spirit), who man was created to be (spirit, soul, and body), what happened to cause man to change, the result of that change, what God did to bring man back to his original state, and the current state of man.

Who Is the Godhead?

Who is God? What is meant by Godhead? Why is it important to know about God and the Godhead? Knowing about God is important for living our lives, since He created us. However, knowing about God is not enough. We must know God (especially since we were created by God and in his image and likeness). We must go beyond knowing about God to truly knowing Him (having a personal relationship with Him). We turn our knowledge about God into knowledge of God by turning each truth that we learn about God into matter for meditation before God, leading to prayer and praise to God.[3]

We explore who God says He is. Although there is no way to be exhaustive in our knowledge of God, we can lay a foundation that can be strengthened through continued study of God's word. We know that God is triune: there are within the Godhead three persons (the Father, the Son, and the Holy Spirit). The Father purposed redemption, the Son secured redemption, and the Holy Spirit applied redemption.[4]

If mankind is in the image and likeness of God, it is important to know as much about God as possible. This is the only way we will know what we are supposed to be like. The mere fact that God said let *us* make man, means that He was not alone.

After careful research, I found that God is triune (three in one), sometimes referred to as the Godhead. God is one in character and nature with one purpose and goal, but distinct in role and function. Some truths that I know about God from his word are:

---

[3] J. L. Packer, *Knowing God* (Downers Grove: InterVarsity Press, 1973), 23.
[4] Ibid., 20.

> God is love, He is a Spirit, He is the truth, and He is three distinct persons (each God, operating as one).
> God the Father is the planner, the Originator, and the Creator of all things.
> God, in the person of his Son (Jesus Christ, the Word) speaks and carries out the plan of God.
> God's Spirit (Holy Spirit) made man a living being and reveals who Jesus is to the believer.

Each person of the Trinity has different roles. For example, in Creation:

> The Father spoke the creation into being (Genesis 1:3, 6, 9, 11, 14, 20, 24).
> God the Son carried out the decrees: "All things were made through him, and without him was not anything made that was made" (John 1:3).
> God the Holy Spirit was present at creation: "And the Spirit of God was hovering over the face of the waters" (Genesis 1:2).

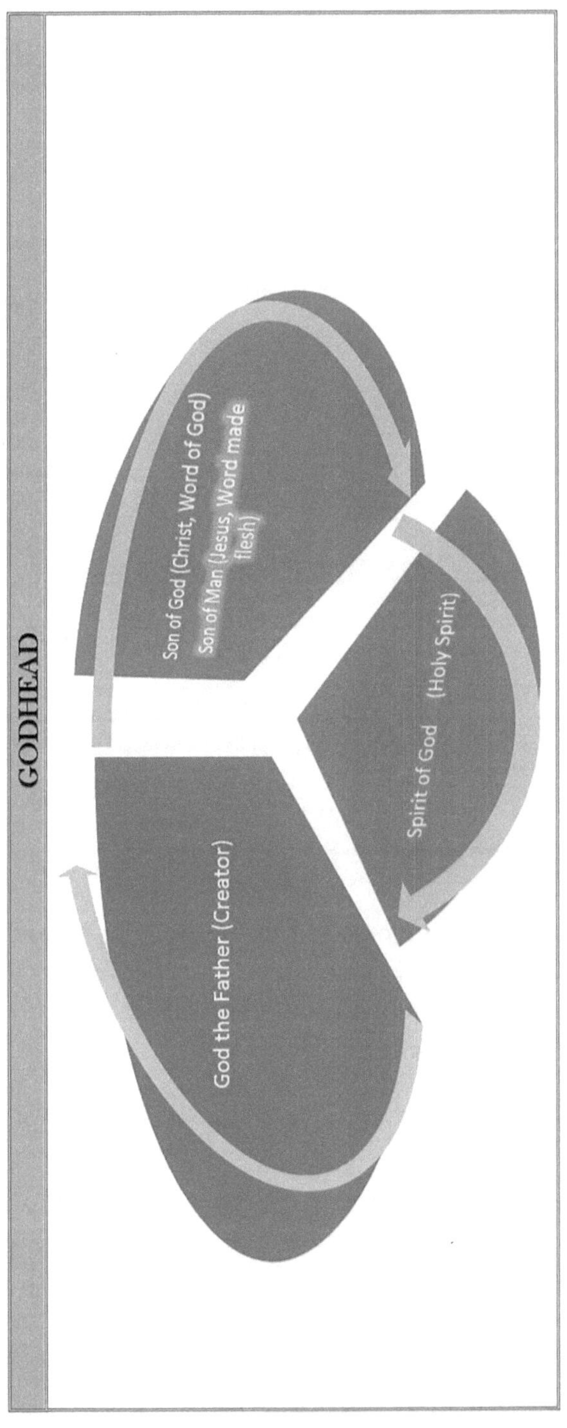

GODHEAD
Son of God (Christ, Word of God)
Son of Man (Jesus, Word made flesh)
Spirit of God   (Holy Spirit)
God the Father (Creator)

In the great commission, Jesus tells the disciples what is expected of them when he ascends into heaven. There are some things that we know about God: *God is love* (1 John 4:8), *God is a Spirit* (John 4:24), *God is divine* (Isaiah 40:28), *God is a person* (John 1:1, 14).

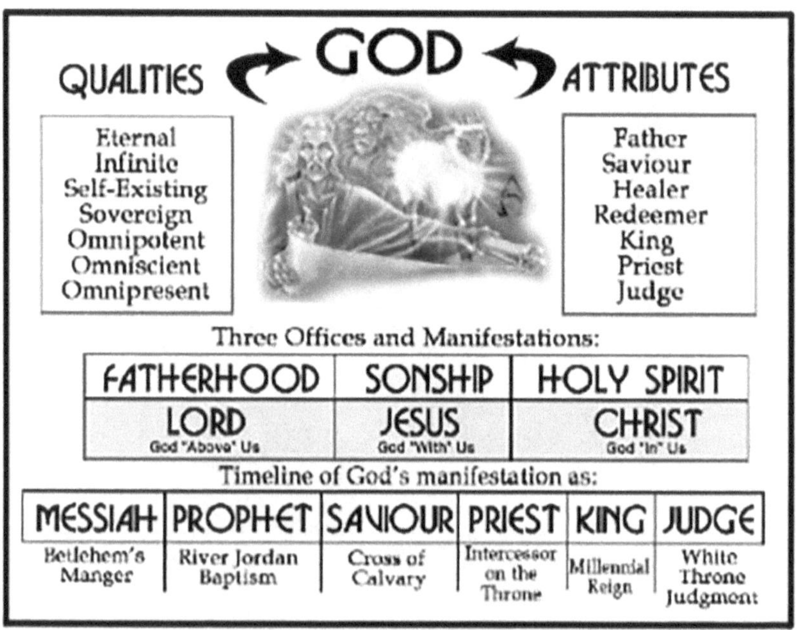

I can of mine own self do nothing: as I hear, I judge: and my judgment is just; because I seek not mine own will, but the will of the Father which hath sent me. (John 5:30)

I and *my* Father are one. (John 10:30)

Jesus saith unto him, I am the way, *the truth*, and the life: no man cometh unto the Father, but by me...he that hath seen me hath seen the Father; and how sayest thou *then,* Shew us the Father? (John_14:6, 9)

> For there are three that bear record in heaven, *the Father, the Word, and the Holy Ghost: and these three are one.* (1 John 5:7)

When we were first created, we were spirit beings. Our spirit had God's nature because his spirit was blown into our nostrils to give us life. *We were in the image and likeness of God,* so just as *He is a triune being, we are made of three parts. We are spirit beings. We have a soul* (comprised of our mind, our will, and our emotions), and *we live in a body.* When you look at me, you are not seeing the real me because my spirit cannot be seen. We initially had authority/dominion over every living thing on earth (notice that God gave rule/dominion over animals, not mankind).

Mankind

From the beginning of creation, mankind was created in the image and likeness of God. This meant that mankind was in the kingdom of God at creation.

Genesis 1 and 2 explains to us that mankind (male and female) was created by God, and everything that God created was very good. There was no knowledge of good and evil when man was first created. He was created to fellowship with the Father. The only thing mankind was to do was replenish the earth. He had only been given instructions to eat of everything in the garden, except fruit from the tree of life and the tree of the knowledge of good and evil.

Since mankind was made in the image and likeness of God, had he not disobeyed God, he would have continued to have dominion of the earth. He was able to speak things into existence, just as his Father. Since Adam and Eve were the first and only humans created, it means that we all came from Adam. Therefore, it is insane to assume oneself better than or less than another human being. Initially, mankind was ruled by the Spirit of God since he had no knowledge of good and evil.

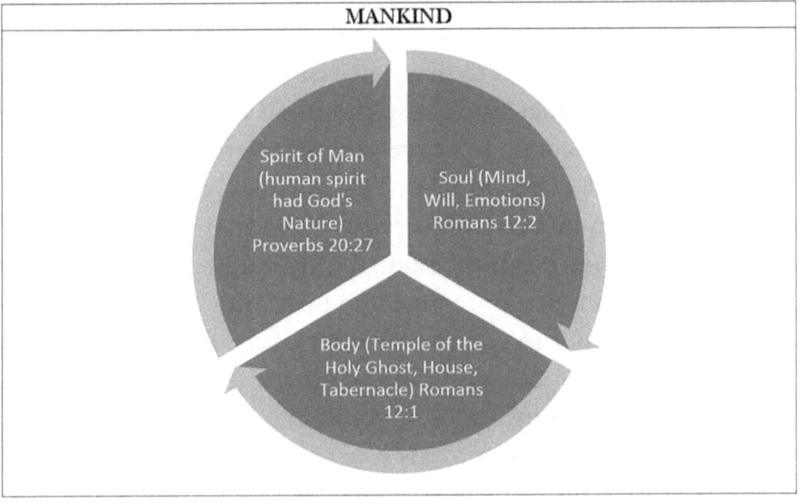

MANKIND
Spirit of Man (human spirit had God's Nature) Proverbs 20:27
Soul (Mind, Will, Emotions) Romans 12:2
Body (Temple of the Holy Ghost, House, Tabernacle) Romans 12:1

Mankind and the Fall

I have often wondered since childhood that if everything that God created was good, how did we end up in the condition we are in? As an African American female, it has taken every ounce of faith within me to continue believing that God loves me, protects me, and provides for me. It was really an eye-opening experience when I finally understood what it meant to be created in the image of God.

Remembering that God is a spirit helped me to understand that we, too, are spirit beings. You have probably noticed that sometimes when you view a deceased loved one in the casket, they do not resemble themselves. Even as a glove needs a hand in it for movement to occur, so too a body needs the human spirit for life to exist.

The first man, Adam, represented humanity. When he was created, he was told not to eat from the tree of the knowledge of good and evil. When he disobeyed God and ate the fruit, he died. He did not die physically, he instead died spiritually (i.e., the spirit of God which had been breathed into his spirit was replaced with the spirit of satan—evil). This death meant that mankind became separated from God, his Creator. Man's disobedience caused a separation that came with many other penalties:

- Mankind gave his dominion of the earth over to satan (who came in the form of a serpent and deceived Eve).
- When Adam was created (Genesis 1:27), his body was formed (Genesis 2:7), and woman was made from a part of man (Genesis 2:22); they were both naked and unashamed (Genesis 2:25). After Adam disobeyed God, their eyes were opened to their nakedness. "He *is* naked. Of course, that has nothing to do with clothing. He is *'erom*, bare,

exposed, from the verb *'ur*, "to lay bare, to expose." Adam is aware that he is *vulnerable*. For the first time in his life, he is aware of a threat to his existence. He is not safe. That's why he hides!"[5]

When God gave Adam instructions to not eat of the tree of the knowledge of good and evil, his disobedience was the beginning of humanity's knowing what evil was. This was the beginning of man experiencing the evils of the world (man became aware of good and evil). Satan had gained dominion of the world legally because Adam gave up his right to dominion when he disobeyed God's instructions. The *blame* game began with Adam blaming his wife, Eve; and Eve blaming the serpent (Genesis 3:12–13). The entrance of *shame* into man's psyche began, and mankind hid himself from God, attempting to cover himself with manmade covering (fig leaves, Genesis 3:10). The first *murder* occurred when Cain murdered his brother Abel (Genesis 4:9). From that day to this day, mankind was born into the world with a sin nature (shattered innocence), rather than the nature of God.

God is a just God. At any point, He had the power to strip satan of his power. However, because God is just and had given dominion of the earth to man, legally the earth was no longer under his dominion. Since Adam tasted from the tree of the knowledge of good and evil, he began to know evil, and evil has been a part of human nature ever since.

God is good, so even in man's disobedience, God had a plan to restore man back to Himself. However, the consequences of Adam's disobedience are still felt today. Maybe you think this is cruel. However, think about your children. You love them, so if you know something will hurt them, you give instructions telling them not to do it. However, if your child chooses to disobey you, when they get hurt, you didn't cause the hurt to them, hurt came because they disobeyed your instructions. Our Father God is our heavenly Father,

---

5   Skip Moen, "Grace Arrives," Hebrew Word Study, accessed October 9, 2017, https://www.skipmoen.com/2017/10/grace-arrives/.

even as we have a natural father. When we understand that the Father loves us and would never tell us something that would hurt us, it makes it easier to trust Him and joyfully obey Him.

Eve was deceived, but Adam was in disobedience because God had given the instructions to Adam. His disobedience caused his nature to take on the nature of satan (sin nature), instead of the original nature of God. This brought about two kingdoms and two natures: kingdom of light (kingdom of God) with the nature of God, and kingdom of darkness (kingdom of this world) with a sin nature (satan).

Mankind, as a race of people, was created with God's nature inside; however, after mankind disobeyed God (described in section two) we took on the nature of satan. "Whosoever is born of God doth not commit sin; for his seed remaineth in him: and he cannot sin, because he is born of God" (1 John 3:9, KJV). Since the fall, man has to *choose* God in order to regain the nature of God (hence, being born again).

Notice that sin in this passage refers to the sin nature, not the action of sin (sins). The spirit of man takes on God's nature when we accept Jesus as our Lord and Savior. However, as we learned in section 2, man still has to submit his soul and his body to his spirit (which is yielded to the Spirit of God) in order for us to "look like and act like Christ." This happens as we continue to renew our minds with the truth of God's word and submit our bodies (which houses our human spirit) to the Spirit of God (Romans 12:1–2).

When World's Collide

Two Natures—Two Kingdoms

We continually ask God to fill you with the knowledge of his will
through all the wisdom and understanding that the Spirit gives,
so that you may live a life worthy of the Lord and please him
in every way: bearing fruit in every good work, growing in the
knowledge of God, being strengthened with all power according
to his glorious might so that you may have great endurance
and patience, and giving joyful thanks to the Father, who has
qualified you to share in the inheritance of his holy people in
the *kingdom of light. For he has rescued us from the dominion
of darkness* and brought us into the kingdom of the Son he
loves, in whom we have redemption, the forgiveness of sins.

—Colossians 1:9–14

The Word of God (Bible) is filled with scriptures that reveal the existence of two kingdoms: the kingdom of darkness (satan's rule, ignorance of God, spiritual darkness) and the kingdom of light (God's rule). Kingdom means "the king's domain." The kingdom of God is God's sovereign rule over all of creation. It is a literal, spiritual dimension accessible only to born-again believers.

However, the kingdom is for all humanity, not just believers. Every kingdom has a king whose subjects are required to submit to his rule and whose land reveals his splendor.[6] The kingdom of God is the sovereign rule of God over all of creation.

> For the kingdom of God is not a matter of eating and drinking, but of righteousness, peace and joy in the Holy Spirit, because anyone who serves Christ in this way is pleasing to God and receives human approval. (Romans 14:17–18, NIV)

The kingdom of heaven is God's rule through man on the earth. In the kingdom of heaven, the Lord Jesus Christ is King of kings and Lord of lords. Everything that we need for kingdom living is found in the Word of God (Bible). The phrase "King of kings" implies subordinates to a King. Every earthly king and kingdom has limited power and control; however, there is only one King that is sovereign (Jesus Christ, King of kings). When we know who we are in Christ Jesus, then we take our rightful positions and exercise our kingdom authority in the earth.

> "I will give you the keys (authority) *of* the *kingdom of heaven*; and whatever you bind [forbid, declare to be improper and unlawful] on earth will have [already] been bound in *heaven*, and whatever you loose [permit, declare lawful] on earth will have [already] been loosed in *heaven*." (Matthew 16:19, AMP)

The sovereignty of God does not mean that God commands control of everything that happens on earth. In his sovereignty, God chose to make mankind the manager/steward over the earth realm. However, when man disobeyed God and listened to satan instead, he lost dominion of the earth and satan became his god and god of this world. That is why it is important for every believer to:

---

[6] Cindy Trimm, *Understanding the Kingdom* (Trimm Media Group, 2015).

> First *and* most importantly seek (aim at, strive
> after) His (God's) kingdom and His righteousness
> [His way of doing and being right—the attitude
> and character of God], and all these things will
> be given to you also. (Matthew 6:33, AMP)

> But even if our gospel is [in some sense] hidden
> [behind a veil], it is hidden [only] to those who
> are perishing; among them the god of this world
> [satan] has blinded the minds of the unbeliev-
> ing to prevent them from seeing the illuminating
> light of the gospel of the glory of Christ, who is
> the image of God. (2 Corinthians 4:3–4, AMP)

Our King is a sovereign King. Sovereignty has been misunderstood to mean controlling everything. While God is the Creator of
all things, He chose to given dominion of the earth to mankind,
who, through disobedience, relinquished it to satan. However, God
(through Jesus) won dominion back and made kingdom living avail-
able to all who accepted Jesus as their King, Lord, and Savior.

It still remains a matter of choice as to who becomes the king
of our lives. We decide whom we want to be Lord of our lives. Every
king in the universe falls under God's jurisdiction. Our citizen-
ship is not of this world, but of another kingdom. Upon salvation,
the believer becomes a citizen of the kingdom of light and benefits from its numerous privileges. Dr. Cindy Trimm, in her course
Understanding the Kingdom, compares the United States and God's
Kingdom.

THE KING AND HIS KINGDOM[7]		
	USA	**GOD'S KINGDOM**
Origins	• The American Revolution 1776 • Declaration of Independence	• Jesus's incarnation, crucifixion and death, resurrection, and ascension; the Holy Spirit's coming at Pentecost • Declaration of utter dependence on Jesus, interdependence on our Christian brothers and sisters, and independence from satan
Territory	• Part of North America, including Hawaii, and a few other islands • Capital in Washington DC	• In heaven with a branch on earth • In the hearts of people of all nations (see Luke 17:21)
Becoming a Citizen	• By being born of US parents • By living in the US for the requisite amount of time, passing a citizenship test	• By rebirth through faith in Christ (John 3:3, 5)
Government	• Three branches: executive, legislative, judicial	• Three persons in God: the Holy Trinity working through the Church
Leadership	• Only a few citizens are leaders who are elected by the vote of the people, except for the appointment of some judges and executive branch leaders	• All citizens are leaders elected by God
Legal System	• The Constitution, the Bill of Rights, and other legislation passed by Congress, state, and city	• The laws of the church and the Bible

---

7. Trimm, Cindy Dr., Understanding the Kingdom, Kingdom School of Ministry ©2015

Law Enforcement	• Apprehension and punishment of offenders through the police, the judicial system, and prisons	• Love for offenders expressed in conviction, forgiveness, and mercy
Foreign Policy	• Based on military strength and diplomacy	• No military army, but a spiritual army (Ephesians 6:12) • Both a servant to other governments and a sign of contradiction to them (Luke 2:34)
Economy	• Capitalism	• Christian stewardship, community sharing, and simple lifestyle
Government Finances	• Taxes collected by the government and enforced by the police and judicial system	• By tithes and alms given on the "honor system." There is no collection or enforcement agency
Education	• Public schools run by school board and school superintendent	• Parents as the primary educators; teachers as helpers to parents
Sanctity of Life	• Generally, human life protected from birth to death • Abortion legal	• Human life protected from conception into eternity • Abortion forbidden
Patriotic Symbols	• American eagle • The flag	• The lamb • The cross
The Future	• Will be destroyed	• Will never end

The Word of God (Bible)

The instruction manual for the believer is the Bible (Word of God). The Bible is a record of God's relationship with mankind. The Bible is divided into two parts: the Old Testament (Hebrew Bible, thirty-nine books, written to the Jews) and the New Testament (Greek Bible, twenty-seven books, written to Christians). Some of the New Testament writers were eyewitnesses to what they were writing about.

The Bible is an orderly, progressive, unfolding revelation from God of the blood covenant He made with Himself for us through Jesus. The Bible is the story of an older covenant and a newer covenant (binding agreement between two parties). The two divisions of the Bible are about an old blood covenant and a new blood covenant.

The Old Testament is a picture of God's salvation message in Jesus, in shadow form (rituals, customs, places, names, etc.). A shadow is not the real thing, but it points to the real thing. Every believer in the Old Testament offered an innocent substitutionary sacrifice to cover their sins and point them into the future when God Himself, through Jesus, would come and take away their sins. The Old Testament foretells the happenings of the crucifixion and resurrection, but the New Testament records that the crucifixion and resurrection happened. God revealed his covenant to Adam and Eve after they had sinned. He gives the first promise of redemption and a preview of his plan of atonement for sin through the blood of the everlasting covenant.[8] As God said to satan:

---

8. Richard Booker, *Discovering the Miracle of the Scarlet Thread in Every Book of the Bible* (Destiny Image Publishing, Inc, 1983).

> And I will put enmity (open hostility) between
> you and the woman,
> And between your seed (offspring) and her Seed;
> He shall [fatally] bruise your head, and you shall
> [only] bruise His heel. (Genesis 3:15, AMP)

The Holy Spirit simply dictated the account of God's relationship with his people, Israel. The accounts in the Bible is a record of the good, the bad, and the ugly. Everything in the Bible is truly stated, but not everything in the Bible is a statement of truth. It is truly stated that Job said, "The Lord gave, and the Lord has taken away." However, Job 1:6–12 reveals that this is not a statement of truth. Job attributes his loss to God, but Job opened the door to satan through his fear of what might happen: "For the thing which I greatly fear comes upon me, and that of which I am afraid has come upon me" (Job 3:25). Whenever we don't trust God and do what his words says we are to do, we are open to the devices of satan and we have no defense against him.[9]

John 10:10 reminds us that the thief (satan) comes to steal, kill, and destroy. However, Jesus said that He came that we might have life and have life more abundantly. James 1:7 tells us that every good and every perfect gift comes down from the Father of Light. Therefore, we must study God's Word, meditate on the Word, and rightly divide God's Word (the word of truth).

Revelation of God is progressive. God reveals more facets of his plan for mankind as knowing the character of God will help in knowing the truth about what we are reading in the Word. We must study God's word in context, always asking who it is written to (i.e., Jews, Christians, unbelievers, Romans, etc.). After salvation, our *spirit is recreated*, but our soul and body are our responsibility. Only God's Word can save our souls (mind, will, and emotions). We must *renew our minds with the word of God* and *present our bodies* as living sacrifices before God.

[9.] Frederick Price, *The Truth About the Bible* (Faith One Publishing, 1999).

So get rid of all uncleanness and all that remains of wickedness, and with a humble spirit receive the word [of God] which is implanted [actually rooted in *your* heart], which is *able to save your souls*. But prove yourselves doers of the word [actively and continually obeying God's precepts], and not merely listeners [who hear the word but fail to internalize its meaning], deluding yourselves [by unsound reasoning contrary to the truth]. (James 1:21–22, AMP)

Therefore I urge you, brothers and sisters, by the mercies of God, to *present your bodies* [dedicating all of yourselves, set apart] as a living sacrifice, holy and well-pleasing to God, *which is* your rational (logical, intelligent) act of worship. And do not be conformed to this world [any longer with its superficial values and customs], but be transformed *and* progressively changed [as you mature spiritually] by the *renewing of your mind* [focusing on godly values and ethical attitudes], so that you may prove [for yourselves] what the will of God is, that which is good and acceptable and perfect [in His plan and purpose for you]. (Romans 12:1–2, AMP)

The Bible is our guide for living a victorious life in the earth. David said in Psalm 119:105, "Your word is a lamp to my feet, and a light to my path."

A Matter of Choice

God in his omnipotence, omniscience, and omnipresence was everywhere, all-powerful, all-seeing, and all-knowing. However, He chose to work in cooperation with man. Since man had legally given up his dominion, God would have to regain the dominion legally. God can do no evil, and therefore, He would restore his relationship with mankind justly. Being the loving God that He is, He gave mankind the ability to choose what he wanted. Even as God told the children of Israel, He is saying to us today, "This day I call the heavens and the earth as witnesses against you that *I have set before you life and death, blessings and curses. Now choose life*, so that you and your children may live" (Deuteronomy 30:19, NIV).

Choosing life means that we choose to do things the way God says to do them rather than the way of the world. When I see racism, rape, murder, selfishness, and other things that destroy lives, I understand that all these ills of the world are a result of someone choosing death rather than life; evil rather than good. Unfortunately, the choices that others make may also impact our lives, just as our choices impact other people's lives. Many times, we accuse God of things that He is not responsible for. After the fall of Adam, we live in a fallen world, and when we disobey God's word, although He grants us his grace, there are still consequences for our disobedience.

No need to panic! God's intention for mankind has never changed. He is still almighty, the Lord of heaven and earth. However, dominion was legally given over to satan. Therefore, God sent Jesus (his Son, the Word made flesh) into the earth as a man. Since a man had lost dominion, it took a man to regain that dominion. However, there was no perfect man on the earth; only God himself could pay the penalty for our sin nature and regain mankind's authority.

Jesus's crucifixion paid for our sins; however, his resurrection gave us authority to do all things through and in his name.

> For if by the trespass of the one (Adam), *death* reigned through the one (Adam), much more *surely* will those who receive the abundance of grace *and* the free gift of righteousness reign in [eternal] *life* through the One, Jesus Christ. (Romans 5:17, AMP)

Though satan no longer has control of the believer, except it is given to him through disobedience, he can deceive people into releasing the authority of their lives to him. He also blinds the minds of unbelievers so that they cannot see how much God loves them. He knows that it is difficult to trust someone that you don't believe loves you.

> *Satan, who is the god of this world,* has blinded the minds of those who don't believe. They are unable to see the glorious light of the Good News. They don't understand this message about the glory of Christ, who is the exact likeness of God. (2 Corinthians 4:4, NLT)

Blinding the minds of those who don't believe in God and the finished works of Jesus is what satan has been doing since the beginning of time. He has always found ways to convince people that God is not who He says He is through deception. Even among believers, he uses deception to keep them from renewing their minds with the word of God, so we become carnal Christians. Although our spirit man is recreated, we are still being controlled by our flesh since we are not renewing our minds with his word and submitting to the lordship of Jesus Christ.

Whether a carnal Christian or an unbeliever, we do not have the mind of Christ unless we feed on his word. The mind of Christ says there is no division.

> There is [now no distinction in regard to salvation] neither Jew nor Greek, there is neither slave nor free, there is neither male nor female; for you [who believe] are all one in Christ Jesus [no one can claim a spiritual superiority). (Galatians 3:28, AMP)

If you really keep the royal law found in Scripture, "Love your neighbor as yourself," you are doing right. But if you show favoritism, you sin and are convicted by the law as lawbreakers. James 2:8-9

It is understandable why an unbeliever would be racist, prejudiced, or biased. However, for the believer, it simply means that spiritual maturity is a matter of choice. A choice to do things God's way regardless of culture or trends. We cannot continue to excuse ourselves for our ancestor's sins, we are accountable to God for our own actions today. Racism is divisive and not of God.

New Creation

Therefore if anyone is in Christ [that is, grafted in, joined to Him by faith in Him as Savior], *he is* a *new* creature [reborn and renewed by the Holy Spirit]; the old things [the previous moral and spiritual condition] have passed away. Behold, *new* things have come [because spiritual awakening brings a *new* life].

—2 Corinthians 5:17 (AMP)

For neither is circumcision anything [of any importance], nor uncircumcision, but [only] a *new creation* [which is the result of a *new* birth—a spiritual transformation—a *new* nature in Christ Jesus].

—Galatians 6:15 (AMP)

I had finally begun to see the light! It seemed too late, after sixty-two years of feeling betrayed by God. I wondered how I could trust God when my entire world seemed to scream that He was not concerned about me. Regardless of how I felt, I knew in my heart that this was a lie.

As a little girl, I had been told that Jesus was my only way to live a victorious life. However, I kept hearing words that I did not understand (saved, born-again, salvation, eternal life, etc.). When Adam disobeyed God, he became spiritually separated from God and inherited the nature of the one he submitted to (satan, a sin nature). When we accept Jesus as our Savior, we choose to renounce our sinful nature and, by faith in Jesus Christ, take on the intended nature of God before the fall. We become new creations in Christ Jesus with all the rights and privileges that were afforded Adam before the fall.

> But what does it say? "THE WORD IS NEAR YOU, IN YOUR MOUTH AND IN YOUR HEART"—THAT IS, THE WORD [THE MESSAGE, THE BASIS] OF FAITH WHICH WE PREACH—BECAUSE IF YOU ACKNOWLEDGE *and* confess with your mouth that Jesus is Lord [recognizing His power, authority, and majesty as God], and believe in your heart that God raised Him from the dead, *you will be saved.* (Romans 10:8–9, AMP)

This passage became clearer to me as I began to study God's word. I suddenly understood that I was reconciled back to God when I accepted Jesus as my Savior. Jesus, as a perfect man, had paid the price for the sin nature I had inherited because of Adam's disobedience. I found that simply joining a church was not the same as salvation. While it is important to become a member—join a local body (church)—it is not the same as salvation. Salvation is defined as:

> The spiritual and eternal deliverance granted immediately by God to those who accept His conditions of repentance and faith in the Lord Jesus, in whom alone it is to be obtained, and upon confession of Him as Lord. For this purpose, the gospel is the saving instrument of the present experience of God's power to deliver from the bondage of sin.[10]

This salvation that took place when I accepted Jesus as my Savior meant that I had a recreated spirit. I now had the Spirit of God dwelling in me again, instead of the nature of satan (sinful nature).

---

10. W. E. Vine, *Vine's Expository Dictionary of Old and New Testament Words* (Thomas Nelson, 1996).

What? know ye not that *your body is the temple of the Holy Ghost* which is in you, which ye have *of* God, and ye are not your own? (1 Corinthians 6:19)

Study of God's word revealed that I could make Jesus my Savior, without making Him the Lord of my life. Just as I chose to accept Jesus as my Savior by faith, I must decide to allow Him to be the Lord of my life by renewing my mind with his word, being a doer of the word, and presenting my body as a living sacrifice to Him daily.

As years went on, I searched for the truth in God's word, only to find that whenever God wanted something done on the earth, He used a man to carry out his plan. I recognized that I and other believers are given the authority for which we have been waiting for God to handle. A revelation of who I really am in Christ Jesus continues to make the world of difference in how I see my life, live my life, and relate to other people.

SECTION 3

God, USA, and Mankind

United States of America (USA)

To better understand myself and the world in which I live, I had to look at the history of our nation. I firmly believe that the USA is a nation blessed by God. The statement *"in God we trust"* on our coins represents a nation that at least acknowledges God. However, because of so many satanic contradictions in my own reality, it became necessary for me to determine how I could successfully navigate life as an African American woman in the USA. This required me to investigate our nation's history, try to understand our nation considering God's word, and understand how to live life victoriously and be a blessing to others in this nation plagued by a racial divide.

The United States is relatively young by world standards, being less than 250 years old; it achieved its current size only in the mid-twentieth century. *America was the first of the European colonies to separate successfully from its motherland,* and it was the first nation to be established on the premise that sovereignty rests with its citizens and not with the government. In its first century and a half, the country was mainly preoccupied with its own territorial expansion and economic growth and with social debates that ultimately *led to civil war and a healing period that is still not complete.* In the twentieth century, the United States emerged as a world power, and it has been one of the preeminent powers since World War II.[11]

For the most part, the English colonies of North America were business ventures. The colonies provided an outlet for England's surplus population and (in some cases) more religious freedom than

---

[11.] Oscar Handlin, Warren Hassler, Harold Bradley, Frank Freidel, Karl Schmidt, James Harris, "United States," Encyclopedia Britannica, https://www.britannica.com/place/United-States.

England did, but their primary purpose was to make money for their sponsors.[12]

United, is defined by Webster's dictionary as "made one (combined), relating to or produced by joint action, a united effort, agreeing (harmonious)." From its inception, God's hand was upon the USA. Being "one" was not a concept that originated with our nation. God Himself said the same thing when *He created* mankind (male and female), and instituted marriage. Genesis 2:24 says, "Therefore shall a man leave his father and his mother and shall cleave unto his wife: and *they shall be one flesh.*"

United States, officially United States of America, abbreviated US or USA, byname America, country in North America, a federal republic of fifty states. Besides the forty-eight conterminous states that occupy the middle latitudes of the continent, the United States includes the state of Alaska at the northwestern extreme of North America and the island state of Hawaii in the mid-Pacific Ocean.[13]

United States (states united), what a powerful concept, suggesting no division. The Pledge of Allegiance resonates the words *"one nation under God, indivisible, with liberty and justice for all."* What was their definition of "all"? Since many held a belief that African Americans were not human, their perception may have been unjust from its foundation. These words indicate a foundation upon which decent men chose to recognize God. "If the foundations be destroyed, what can the righteous do?" (Psalms 11:3, KJV). Matthew 12:25 states, "A house divided against itself shall not stand." Whether it be nations, states, families, or individuals, division is a sure way for the enemy to destroy us all or assist us in destroying one another. The old familiar adage "divide and conquer" is one of the enemy's greatest strategies for the defeat of nations, families, and individuals.

United suggests unity, no division. The phrase "United We Stand, Divided We Fall" was a phrase whose origin was not in the USA. Although a common motto used on our flags and other

---

[12.] "The 13 Colonies," History, http://www.history.com/topics/thirteen-colonies.

[13.] Handlin, Hassler, Bradley, Freidel, Schmidt, Harris, "United States" https://www.britannica.com/place/United-States.

emblems, the phrase is traced back to Aesop, a Greek storyteller in the sixth century. The fable is called "The Four Oxen and the Lion" and reads as follows:

> A lion used to prowl about a field in which four oxen used to dwell. Many a time he tried to attack them; but whenever he came near they turned their tails to warn another, so that whichever way he approached them he was met by the horns of one of them. At last, however, they fell a-quarrelling [*sic*] among themselves, and each went off to pasture alone in the separate corner of the field. Then the Lion attacked them one by one and soon made an end of all four. *United we stand, divided we fall.*[14]

The fable suggests that the lion was unable to destroy his prey if they worked together (unified). However, when they became divided and alone, the lion attacked each ox one by one until all were destroyed. From inception, the United States was divided among the Southern states and the Northern states. The states were divided in their beliefs on the enslavement of African human beings. The same colonists that fought for their independence from British rule could not understand why another human being would want to be independent and free.

---

14. Aesop, "The Four Oxen and the Lion," *Fables*, Bartleby, http://www.bartleby.com/17/1/52.html.

God and the USA

The LORD FOILS THE PLANS OF THE NATIONS; HE THWARTS THE PURPOSES OF THE PEOPLES.... *Blessed is the nation whose God is the* LORD; *and* the people *whom* he hath chosen for his own inheritance.

—Psalm 33:10, 12 (NIV)

Although the verses above applied to Old Testament children of Israel, God's word is still valid today and applies to us today. In a culture where "God" means different things to different people, "God" in this book refers to the Almighty Creator of the universe in the person of the Trinity (Father, Son, and Holy Spirit). Political correctness and religious tolerance has made "God" to be whatever the opinion of the person speaking. It is this disregard for God that has caused man to lose his compass, and therefore he has no guide to govern his conscience. Romans 1:22 says it this way: "Professing themselves to be wise, they became fools."

Religion played a central role in the emergence of a distinctively "American" society in the first years of independence. Several key developments took place. One was the creation of American denominations independent of their British and European origins and leadership. By 1789, American Anglicans (renaming themselves Episcopalians), Methodists (formerly Wesleyans), Roman Catholics, and members of various Baptist, Lutheran, and Dutch Reformed congregations had established organizations and chosen leaders who were born in or full-time residents of what had become the United States of America.[15]

[15.] "Religious Revivalism," Encyclopedia Britannica, https://www.britannica.com/place/United-States/Religious-revivalism.

Many say that our nation was not founded on Christian princi-ples. In an article entitled "Founding Fathers: We Are Not a Christian Nation" by Jeff Schweitzer, John Adams is quoted as saying, "The government of the United States is not, in any sense, founded on the Christian religion." Schweitzer further states in his article, "I tremble in fear for my country when the majority of conservatives believe we are a Christian nation; that frightening majority has forgotten our history, ignored our founding principles and abandoned our most cherished ideal of separating church and state. In mixing religion and politics, the religious right subverts both. And the world suffers."[16]

I understand perfectly why Schweitzer would tremble in fear at the thought of mixing religion and politics. However, this and other articles seem to suggest that many of the Founding Fathers were reli-gious. It should be noted at this time that *"religion" and "relationship"* will yield different results, hence explaining many of the problems that we encounter in our culture today.

I, on the other hand, as an African American woman born in the South in the mid-1950s tremble at the thought of this nation attempting to succeed without the guidance of Almighty God. "The fool hath said in his heart, *There is* no God. They are corrupt, they have done abominable works, *there is* none that doeth good" (Psalm 14:1, KJV).

Separation of state may have been taken out of context. Its orig-inal meaning was not to suggest that religion should not play a role in politics, but instead was contained in a letter from Thomas Jefferson in 1802 to Danbury Baptist Association. In the letter, Jefferson sought to protect the right of citizens.

> Believing with you that religion is a matter
> which lies solely between Man & his God, that
> he owes account to none other for his faith or
> his worship, that the legitimate powers of gov-

---

16. Jeff Schweizer, "Founding Fathers: We Are Not A Christian Nation," HuffPost (2015), http://www.huffingtonpost.com/jeff-schweitzer/founding-fathers-we-are-n_b_6761840.html.

ernment reach actions only, & not opinions, I contemplate with sovereign reverence that act of the whole American people which declared that their legislature should "make no law respecting an establishment of religion, or prohibiting the free exercise thereof," thus building a wall of separation between Church & State. Adhering to this expression of the supreme will of the nation in behalf of the rights of conscience, I shall see with sincere satisfaction the progress of those sentiments which tend to restore to man all his natural rights, convinced he has no natural right in opposition to his social duties.[17]

I have seen firsthand how a people respond when they have no true relationship with Jesus Christ. Although I was spared the inhumane treatment that my ancestors faced during slavery, the repercussions of the sin of slavery continues to haunt this nation through racism, color bias, discrimination, and all kinds of inequities.

Slavery was a sin committed by the United States on a people whose only guilt was the color of their skin. Although the United States formally apologized for its actions in institutionalized slavery and the Jim Crow laws, it is simply the first step in the healing process. To begin the healing process, we must acknowledge our wrong; however, repentance (turning away from sin) is the next step. This can only be done when hearts are changed. No man can change his own heart. He must accept Jesus as his Lord and Savior, yield to the truth of God's word, submit his will to God's will, and allow the Word of God to transform his mind.

Few things comprised the core values of the US Constitution and left as lasting a mark on American society as 246 years of institutionalized slavery and the subsequent discriminating of the Jim Crow

---

[17.] Thomas Jefferson, "Jefferson's Letter to the Danbury Baptists: The Final Letter, as Sent," Library of Congress, accessed August 7, 2010, https://www.loc.gov/loc/lcib/9806/danpre.html.

laws that marked African Americans as second-class citizens. As such, few people were more deserving of a formal apology than the millions of black Americans whose ancestors were forcibly brought to this country and had their freedom stolen from them.

The formal apology for slavery and Jim Crow issued by the US House of Representatives in 2008 was unprecedented, even after decades of lawmakers trying to push the government to finally apologize. While the apology was primarily symbolic, by officially recognizing its role in perpetuating the horrors of slavery and Jim Crow, the American government took a step forward in addressing and atoning for one of its greatest wrong.[18]

The nation symbolically apologized; however, many individuals still hold to the values of institutionalized slavery, racism, discrimination, etc. Anyone who knows the character of God knows that He never forces Himself on anyone; He simply offers us a choice. Even in our secular society, we know that consequences come because of the choices we make. God simply tells us that He can show us a better way to handle things than our self-centered means of decision-making.

I would say to myself and any skeptics, please do not judge God based on the behavior of people. Invite God to reveal Himself to you personally, and He will send the right people your way. I myself remind myself that my focus is on becoming more intimate with God. If I lose that focus, the verdict that I would give would not be good, if there is any truth to reaping what you have sown.

The United States is a government of the people, by the people, for the people. Many believe that this statement was coined by President Lincoln in his Gettysburg Address; however, this statement was borrowed from John Wycliff's translation of the Bible in 1384 that states, "The Bible is for the Government of the People, by the People, and for the People." Lincoln did, however, enshrine the people's rule in the fervent pledge that, "under God," this democracy shall not perish from the earth.[19] This concept of government is great

---

[18] Danny Lewis, "Five Times the United States Officially Apologized," Smithsonian, accessed May 27, 2016, http://www.smithsonian.com.

[19] "Who Coined 'Government of the People, By the People, For the People," Washington Post, accessed March 31, 2017, https://www.washingtonpost.

when of the people, by the people, for the people equally *includes all people.*

Just as we each have an opinion, the trillions of varying opinions in any nation must have a guide to aid in directing those opinions, which impact people's lives. Opinions, which many times are tainted by personal biases, can hinder just decision making. The Word of God (Bible) provides that compass that provides guidance for governing all people as we ourselves would like to be governed. This guide must seek the best for all people, not just those in our circle. I know of no human being that can provide such guidance; only a just God can guide men to be just despite their biases. "The steps of a *good* man are ordered by the LORD: and he delighteth in his way" (Psalm 37:23, KJV). "A man's heart deviseth his way: but the LORD directeth his steps" (Proverbs 16:9).

America became a superpower, not by her own strength and wisdom, but because of seeking God for direction. Rather than becoming wiser than the Creator Himself, many sought God privately for direction. In the Declaration of Independence (July 4, 1776), while the first paragraph alludes to separation between politics and religion, the second paragraph states:

> We hold these truths to be self-evident, that all men are created equal, that they are endowed *by their Creator* with certain unalienable Rights, that among these are Life, Liberty and the pursuit of Happiness. — That to secure these rights, Governments are instituted among Men, deriving their just powers from the consent of the governed, — That whenever any Form of Government becomes destructive of these ends, it is the Right of the People to alter or to abolish it, and to institute new Government, laying its

---

com/opinions/who-coined-government-of-the-people-by-the-people-for-the-people/2017/03/31/12fc465a-0fd5-11e7-aa57-2ca1b05c41b8_story.html?utm_term=.2fb7da90a079,

foundation on such principles and organizing its powers in such form, as to them shall seem most likely to affect their Safety and Happiness.[20]

As children of God, suggesting that we attempt to handle life without the assistance of the one who created us is a violation of religious rights. So, when "Creator" is referenced in the Declaration of Independence, it is an indirect acknowledgment of God as Creator. We know that we are unable to create ourselves. Those who know God and not just know about Him, knows that He is loving, just, and He guides us into all truth (through the Holy Spirit).

A person who is simply religious, attempting life in his own strength with no direction will soon fail. "All the ways of a man *are* clean in his own eyes; but the LORD weigheth the spirits. Commit thy works unto the LORD, and thy thoughts shall be established" (Proverbs 16:2–3). Even as the children of Israel were unable to keep all the laws in the Old Testament, religion alone will not cause a person's heart to change.

We thank God for sending his Son, Jesus, to earth to pay the price for the sin nature of mankind, so that we are no longer required to perform in our strength. Instead, we must seek to accept Jesus as our Lord and Savior, have an intimate relationship with God, renew our minds with the word of God, and present our bodies as a living sacrifice before God. This causes actions to be motivated by the love of God as we are led by his Spirit (rather than our varying opinions). After all, with God, there is no varying. "Jesus Christ the same yesterday, and today, and forever" (Hebrews 13:8, KJV).

Whatever their beliefs, the Founders came from similar religious backgrounds. Most were Protestants. The largest number was raised in the three largest Christian traditions of colonial America— Anglicanism, Presbyterianism, and Congregationalism. Other Protestant groups included the Society of Friends (Quakers), the Lutherans, and the Dutch Reformed. Three Founders were of Roman

---

20. "The Declaration of Independence," USHistory.org, http://www.ushistory.org/declaration/document/.

Catholic heritage. Founders who fall into the category of Christian Deists include Washington (whose dedication to Christianity was clear in his own mind), John Adams, and, with some qualifications, Thomas Jefferson. Jefferson was more influenced by the reason-centered Enlightenment than either Adams or Washington. Orthodox Christians among the Founders include the staunchly Calvinistic Samuel Adams. John Jay (who served as president of the American Bible Society), Elias Boudinot (who wrote a book on the imminent Second Coming of Jesus), and Patrick Henry (who distributed religious tracts while riding circuit as a lawyer) clearly believed in Evangelical Christianity.[21]

The Gettysburg Address (a speech by President Abraham Lincoln during the Civil War at the dedication of Soldiers National Cemetery in Gettysburg, Pennsylvania) had conflicting reports of Lincoln's usage of the phrase "under God." However, the latest copy of the Gettysburg Address clearly shows the usage of "under God."

> Now we are engaged in a great civil war, testing whether that nation, or any nation so conceived and so dedicated, can long endure. We are met on a great battle-field of that war. We have come to dedicate a portion of that field, as a final resting place for those who here gave their lives that that nation might live. It is altogether fitting and proper that we should do this.
>
> But, in a larger sense, we cannot dedicate—we cannot consecrate—we cannot hallow—this ground. The brave men, living and dead, who struggled here, have consecrated it, far above our poor power to add or detract. The world will little note, nor long remember what we say here, but it can never forget what they did here. It is

---

[21] David Holmes, "The Founding Fathers, Deism, and Christianity," Encyclopedia Britannica, accessed December 21, 2006, https://www.britannica.com/topic/The-Founding-Fathers-Deism-and-Christianity-1272214.

for us the living, rather, to be dedicated here to the unfinished work which they who fought here have thus far so nobly advanced. It is rather for us to be here dedicated to the great task remaining before us—that from these honored dead we take increased devotion to that cause for which they gave the last full measure of devotion—that we here highly resolve that these dead shall not have died in vain—that this nation, *under God,* shall have a new birth of freedom—and that government of the people, by the people, for the people, shall not perish from the earth.

Abraham Lincoln
November 19, 1863[22]

Whether the USA wants to acknowledge God or not, God has always had people who included Him in our nation's affairs. Some important facts to consider:

- "In God We Trust" was first placed on United States coins in 1861, during the Civil War.
- Teddy Roosevelt tried to remove the words from our money in 1907, but was shouted down.
- Only in 1956 was that expression adopted as the national motto by the Eighty-fourth Congress.
- "Under God" in the pledge of allegiance was inserted only in 1954, when President Eisenhower signed legislation to recognize the dedication of our nation and our people to the Almighty.

Even today, leaders of these United States understand the need to acknowledge God and his activity in our nation. This is shown by

---

[22] Abraham Lincoln, "The Gettysburg Address," Abraham Lincoln Online. http://www.abrahamlincolnonline.org/lincoln/speeches/gettysburg.htm.

the observance of the National Day of Prayer on the first Thursday in May each year.

> *The National Day of Prayer exists to mobilize unified public prayer for America.* The National Day of Prayer is an annual observance held on the first Thursday of May, inviting people of all faiths to pray for the nation. It was created in 1952 by a joint resolution of the United States Congress and signed into law by President Harry S. Truman. Our Task Force is a privately funded organization whose purpose is to encourage participation on the National Day of Prayer. It exists to communicate with every individual the *need for personal repentance and prayer*, to create appropriate materials, and *to mobilize the Christian community to intercede for America's leaders and its families.* The Task Force represents a Judeo-Christian expression of the national observance, based on our understanding that *this country was birthed in prayer and in reverence for the God of the Bible.*[23]

Our political correctness, religious tolerance, and irreverence for God are showing up in our daily lives and society as more people selfishly promote their plans rather than the plan of God. Taking prayer out of schools, accepting white supremacist ideals (directly or indirectly), and many other acts of dishonoring God raises the question: "How is that working for you?" While my circumstances are not ideal, my desire to please God far outweighs what transpires with me here on earth.

---

[23] "National Day of Prayer," http://www.nationaldayofprayer.org/about.

God, USA, and African Descendants

Then God said, "*Let us (Father, Son, Holy Spirit) make man in Our image, according to Our likeness* [not physical, but a spiritual personality and more likeness]; *and let them have complete authority* over the fish of the sea, the birds of the air, the cattle, and over the entire earth, and over everything that creeps and crawls on the earth." So, *God created man in His own image, in the image and likeness of God He created him; male and female created He them.*

—Genesis 1:26–27 (AMP)

God saw *everything that He had made*, and behold, it was *very good, and* He validated it completely. And there was evening and there was morning, a sixth day.

—Genesis 1:31 (AMP)

If a man say, I love God, and hateth his brother, he is a liar: for he that loveth not his brother whom he hath seen, how can he love God whom he hath not seen? And this commandment have we from him, that he who loveth God love his brother also.

—1 John 4:20–21

In the passages above, it is evident that God was the creator of mankind (*all mankind*). Not only did he create mankind (human beings), but *He created us in his image, after his likeness*. Although research shows that there are varying opinions about the institution of slavery, it must be understood that many forms of documentation were written by people who were slave owners, and therefore their perspective had to be tainted by human biases (unless yielded to the "truth"—God's word). Keep in mind also that even God's word was abused by those who *chose* to use it (whether ignorantly or purposefully) for convenience rather than transformation. I have endeavored to seek God's perspective on this troubling issue, since I and this nation need healing. Racism and color bias are direct products of the institution of slavery. *Racism is not from God!*

This section will point out some important facts that I have found in research about the institution of slavery and how we can break the cyclic impact on our society. I accept the historical information provided only as a guide to give me a perspective on how we (as a people) arrived at this point.

The San people of southern Africa, who have lived as hunter-gatherers for thousands of years, are likely to be the oldest population of humans on earth, according to the biggest and most detailed analysis of African DNA. "The project found modern Africans had the most diverse DNA of all racial groups in the world, confirming the idea that *Africa is the birthplace of humanity*," said Sarah Tishkoff of the University of Pennsylvania.[24]

The first Africans taken to Virginia, or at least some of them, appear to have worked as indentured servants. Not until the case of John Punch in the 1640s did it become legally established that black "servants" were to remain such for life. Having escaped, been caught, and brought to trial, *Punch, an indentured servant of African descent, and two other indentured servants of European descent received very different sentences, with Punch's punishment being servitude for the "rest of his natural life"* while that for the other two was merely an extension of their service.[25]

Slavery was not unique to the United States; it is a part of almost every nation's history, from Greek and Roman civilizations to contemporary forms of human trafficking. The American part of the

---

24. Steve Connor, "World's Most Ancient Race Traced in DNA Study," The Independent (2009), https://www.independent.co.uk/news/science/worlds-most-ancient-race-traced-in-dna-study-1677113.html.

25. "The New England Colonies," Encyclopedia Britannica, https://www.britannica.com/place/United-States/The-New-England-colonies.

story lasted fewer than four hundred years. African Americans have been free in this country for less time than they were enslaved. Do the math: blacks have been free for 152 years, which means that most Americans are only two to three generations away from slavery. This is not that long ago. Over this same period, however, *former slaveholding families* have built their legacies on the institution and generated wealth that *African Americans have not had access to because enslaved labor was forced.* Segregation maintained wealth disparities, and overt and covert discrimination limited African American recovery efforts.[26]

In the table below, some key events of the African American timeline of events from 1619 to 2000 in the United States are reflected. As painful as it may be, these events have left bitterness, resentment, hatred, anger, entitlement, inferiority, and many other evil traits in the hearts and minds of the races. A determined effort to change must exist, not by our power and might alone, but by the Spirit of God.

Year	Civil Rights Events
1619	A year before the Mayflower, the first twenty African slaves are sold to settlers in Virginia as indentured servants
1624	The first African American child, William Tucker, is born in the colony
1789	Constitution adopted; slaves counted as three-fifths of a person for means of representation
1831	Nat Turner leads slave revolt in Virginia
1857	Dred Scott sues for his freedom. The Supreme Court rules against him, saying African American people are regarded as "so far inferior…that they had no rights which the white man should respect, and slaves were not citizens"
1861	Civil War begins
1863	Abraham Lincoln signs the Emancipation Proclamation
1865	Civil War Ends. Thirteenth Amendment to the Constitution stating: "neither slavery nor involuntary servitude…shall exist" in the United States

---

[26] Daina Ramey Berry, "Slavery in America: Why Myths and Misconceptions Persist," *Newsweek* (2017), http://www.newsweek.com/slavery-america-popular-misconceptions-627229.

1868	Fourteenth Amendment, making African Americans full citizens in the United States and prohibiting states from denying them equal protection or due process of law. Congress reports that 373 freed slaves have been killed by whites
1870	Fifteenth Amendment enacted, guaranteeing the right to vote will not be denied or abridged on account of race.
1870	The first Jim Crow (segregation law) is passed in Tennessee, mandating separation of African Americans from whites on trains, depots. Other southern states pass similar laws and African Americans are banned from hotels, barber shops, restaurants, theaters and other public accommodations
1875	Congress passes the first Civil Rights Act, guaranteeing African Americans equal rights in transportation/inns, theaters, and on juries. The law is struck down in 1863 with Court majority arguing the Constitution allows Congress to act only on discrimination by government and not that by private citizens
1877	Reconstruction ends, and federal troops are withdrawn from South leaving African Americans no protection and restoration of white supremacy
1890	Constitutional Convention meets to write a suffrage amendment, including poll tax and a literacy test designed successfully to exclude African Americans from voting
1896	The Supreme Court, in Plessy vs. Ferguson rules that state laws requiring separation of the races are within the bounds of the Constitution as long as equal accommodations are made for African American, establishing the "separate but equal" doctrines that justifies legal segregation in the South. *Justice John Harlan, in lone dissent, says Constitution is "colorblind and neither knows nor tolerates classes among citizens"*
1900	Lynching has become virtually a fact of life as a means of intimidating African Americans. Between 1886 and 1900, more than 2,500 lynchings in the nation (mostly in the South)

These are examples of when the nature of a man is not guided by the love of God, he makes himself become a God and seeks his own ways. It should be noted that America is not the only nation that participated in the institution of slavery. However, since people of African descent were the original race, it is clear to me how the enemy used the institution of slavery to plant seeds of inferiority and devalue people of African descent, refusing to acknowledge that we are all related in some way.

> He that loveth his brother abideth in the light,
> and there is none occasion of stumbling in him.
> But he that hateth his brother is in darkness, and
> walketh in darkness, and knoweth not whither
> he goeth, because that darkness hath blinded his
> eyes. (1 John 2:10–11)

The consequences that came because of the inhumane value on African lives remains prominent in America today and can be seen in each of the seven spheres of society: family, economics (science, technology, and business), government, religion, education, media (communication), and celebration (arts, entertainment, and sports).

God's View of Each Sphere of Society:[27]

- *Family*—God is the one who had the original idea of family. He instituted marriage at the very beginning of creation (Genesis 2:24) as the lifetime commitment between one man and one woman. When the original couple expanded into a family with the birth of their first child, we are told that it was "with the LORD's help" (Genesis 4:1). His purpose for this sphere is that life might be multiplied and that a God-given destiny for every individual may be established. God wants us to engage with families, to serve and strengthen them, to see his purposes of life and destiny restored in them to serve an emerging generation. Through the sphere of family, God reveals Himself as Father, Son, and Friend

- *Economy (Science, Technology, and Business)*—God's purpose for the sphere of economics is to release provision and model stewardship. Through the sphere of economics, God wants to reveal Himself as Creator, Provider, and Healer.

---

[27] David Joel Hamilton, *God Revealed Through the Spheres of Society* (2014), https://www.ywam.org/custom-content/uploads/2014/09/God-Revealed-through-the-Spheres-of-Society.pdf.

- *Government*—God has appointed government to safeguard justice and create a peaceful and safe environment within the nation. Rulers should exercise delegated authority to serve the citizens whom they govern. The "Law of the King" found in Deuteronomy 17:14–21 warns those in authority against multiplying that which would lead them into a lifestyle of authoritarianism, hedonism, and materialism. God's alternative to these three unrighteous value systems is servanthood, purity, and generosity. God wants to reveal Himself in this sphere as Lawgiver, Judge, and King.

- *Religion*—God's purpose for the sphere of religion is the extension of mercy and the promotion of reconciliation between those who have had relationships broken. This is to occur horizontally between human beings and vertically between individuals and God. Through the sphere of religion, God wants to reveal Himself as Priest, Prophet, and Intercessor

- *Education*—God has designed the educational sphere to be a means of discipleship and multiplication. The purpose of discipleship is the transformation of the student rather than the mere transaction of knowledge. With this perspective, education becomes a means of developing biblical Christians who have Jesus as their model and the Bible as their foundation. In this sphere, God wants to reveal Himself as Warrior, Shepherd, and Teacher.

- *Media (Communication)*—God's purposes for the sphere of media is the transfer of wisdom and the promotion of healthy relationships. Proverbs is full of pithy axioms that emphasize the power of communication to do good or to do ill. Through this sphere, God wants to reveal Himself as the Way, the Truth, and the Life.

- *Celebration (Arts, Entertainment, and Sports)*—God's purposes for the sphere of celebration is to strengthen hope and build community. Ever since the days of Jubal (Genesis 4:21), balladeers and artists have used their skills to entertain people. Through this sphere, God wants to reveal Himself as source of our Righteousness, Peace, and Joy.

For every revelation of God, there is a counterfeit of the world system. Slavery was a sin committed by people who enslaved other people for their profit. Racism is a product of slavery. Today, in each sphere of society, the repercussions of slavery can be seen. Slavery was one of those counterfeits and had a major impact on the seven spheres of society.

Sphere of Influence	Slavery
Family	Slavery not only inhibited family formation but made stable, secure family life difficult, if not impossible. A father might have one owner; his "wife" and children, another. Family separation through sale was a constant threat.[28]
Economics (Science, Technology, and Business)	*Joseph et al. (2013) found that* slavery represented a thriving business that helped the Southern, more agricultural economy flourish, but also one that had extensive Northern ties. The unpaid labor of enslaved Africans helped build elite universities, and *resources from slavery* were used for campus libraries and to propel university endowments. "The impact of slavery on current income inequality is determined by racial inequality" (Bertocchi Dimico, 2010).
Government	*Joseph et al. (2013) found that* institution's political and psychological assaults on both individuals and the nation's character. Racial segregation's origin story remains firmly rooted in antebellum slavery.
Religion	Except for the Society of Friends, all religious groups in America supported slavery. In the South, black people were not usually allowed to attend church services. One of the main reasons why masters did not want their slaves to become Christians involved the Bible. They feared that slaves might interpret the teachings of Jesus Christ as being in favor of equality. This was one of the main reasons why most plantation owners did what they could to stop their slaves from learning to read.[29]

[28.] Heather A. Williams, "How Slavery Affected African American Families," National Humanities Center, http://nationalhumanitiescenter.org/tserve/freedom/1609-1865/essays/aafamilies.htm.

[29.] "Religion and Slavery," Spartacus Educational, http://spartacus-educational.com/USASreligion.htm.

Sphere of Influence	Slavery
Education	One of the ways slavery affected the people entrapped in its grip was that it inhibited their ability to receive any form of education. In the United States, the effects of hundreds of years of slavery are still being felt.
Media (Communication)	From before the Civil War until today, reporters have exposed slavery's existence. Their stories awakened public awareness to slaves' lives and to the efforts of abolitionists to free them. In the mid-nineteenth century—as the PBS American Experience series *"The Abolitionists"* attests—many of those fighting to abolish slavery (such as William Lloyd Garrison, Angelina Grimké, Harriett Beecher Stowe, and Frederick Douglass) also published newspapers or wrote books to carry forth their message.
Celebration (Arts, Entertainment, and Sports)	The institution of slavery oppressed Africans and African Americans as a people; however, their will to experience a normal setting through cultural entities such as music, religion, and sports is the essential narrative on the accurate story of millions of people who have been lost in one of history's darkest sagas. Sports were a way to not only release built-up emotions and frustrations, but were also a physical escape from the realities of slave life. The athletic and physical thrill of sports, competition, and hunting were pivotal aspects of life for many African American slaves, yet recreational activities stretched far beyond the limits of brute activity and physical athleticism. Historically, the influence of music on the slave community had an impact far beyond being a simple social diversion from cruel reality. While leading hundreds of slaves to freedom through the Underground Railroad, Harriet Tubman used song and music to encode secret messages and meeting places for runaway slaves. Culturally, music had a great impact on slave life in all forms. However, recreationally, the slave's ability to sing and dance provided them with one of the most rewarding experiences while escaping from the day-to-day reality of plantation life. Community events among the slave quarters were a vital form of leisure, which allowed African American slaves the opportunity to coexist within a social environment. Corn shucking events were the most common social gatherings on the southern plantation for the American slave. Resulting in competitions among blacks and whites; the music, normalcy for slaves.

Sphere of Influence	Slavery
	Corn shuckings were primarily held on Saturday evenings and remained one of the best memories for former slaves post-bondage. Numerous slave narratives show evidence that similar parties took place all over the south.[30]

Slavery, and its subsequent parsing of groups of human beings based on race, is at the core of our national identity. Once this is understood, our contemporary circumstances become much clearer, even logical. From this perspective it's quite understandable why reconstruction failed, despite the heroic efforts of African Americans (and at times white allies) to reimagine a new more-inclusive country that had never been in existence.[31]

A new Pew Research Center survey finds profound differences between black and white adults in their views on racial discrimination, barriers to black progress, and the prospects for change. Blacks, far more than whites, say black people are treated unfairly across different realms of life, from dealing with the police to applying for a loan or mortgage. And, for many blacks, racial equality remains an elusive goal. The survey finds that black and white adults have widely different perceptions about what life is like for blacks in the US. For example, by large margins, blacks are more likely than whites to say black people are treated less fairly in the workplace (a difference of forty-two percentage points), when applying for a loan or mortgage (forty-one points), in dealing with the police (thirty-four points), in the courts (thirty-two points), in stores or restaurants (twenty-eight points), and when voting in elections (twenty-three points). By a margin of at least twenty percentage points, blacks are also more likely than whites to say racial discrimination (70% versus 36%), lower quality schools (75% versus 53%), and lack of jobs (66% ver-

---

[30.] Jon Griffith, Sports in Shackles: The Athletic and Recreational Habits of Slaves on Southern Plantations (Voces Novae, 2010), vol. 2, no. 2.

[31.] Peniel E. Joseph, "How Slavery Feeds Todays Racism," The Root (2013), https://www.theroot.com/how-slavery-feeds-todays-racism-1790898665.

sus 45%) are major reasons that blacks may have a harder time getting ahead than whites.

More broadly, blacks and whites offer different perspectives of the current state of race relations in the US. *White Americans are evenly divided, with 46% saying race relations are generally good and 45% saying they are generally bad.* In contrast, by a nearly two-to-one margin, blacks are more likely to say race relations are bad (61%) rather than good (34%). *Blacks are also about twice as likely as whites to say too little attention is paid to race and racial issues in the US these days (58% versus 27%).* About four-in-ten whites (41%)—compared with 22% of blacks—say there is too much focus on race and racial issues.[32]

In families, the African American family is still fragmented. Men have no problem leaving wife and children. In 1965, as an employee of the Office of Policy Planning in the Labor Department during the Johnson Administration, Moynihan released a report called, "The Negro Family: The Case for National Action." Drawing on the work of sociologist *E. Franklin Frazer*, Moynihan traced problems he said African Americans encountered in 1965 back to slavery. Although he acknowledged "a racist virus in the American bloodstream," and noted three centuries of "unimaginable mistreatment," Moynihan blamed what he saw as the disintegration of poor urban black families squarely on slavery. He said slavery had developed a "fatherless matrifocal (mother-centered) pattern" within black families. Men, he claimed, did not learn roles of providing and protecting, and this shortcoming passed down through generations. Moynihan discussed racism and chronic employment and its effects on African Americans, but it was his description of a matrifocal family and its "tangle of pathology" that drew attention both from those who disagreed with him and those who supported his findings.[33]

---

[32] "On Views of Race and Inequality, Blacks and Whites Are Worlds Apart," Pew Research Center (2016), www.pewsocialtrends.org/2016/06/27/on-views-of-race-and-inequality-blacks-and-whites-are-worlds-apart/.

[33] Daniel Patrick Moynihan, "The Negro Family: The Case for National Action," The Moynihan Report (1965), https://www.dol.gov/oasam/programs/history/webid-meynihan.htm.

The poverty that has engulfed the black community ever since it provided the unpaid labor that built American capitalism is the most obvious present-day reverberation of slavery. Institutional racism is also found within our *economic system* through the credit worthiness concept. Many African Americans remain in a cycle of defeat because of discriminatory practices in credit system.

Racial violence, inequality, poverty, mass incarceration, and failing public schools all represent parts of slavery's contemporary legacy. *Judicial system* has institutional racism as "Innocent Until Proven Guilty" only applies to non-minorities. Police automatically assume the worst of an African American, and police brutality ensues. Minorities have very little protection under the law. The *criminal justice system* is the modern-day slavery where many are falsely incarcerated and remain in the system for life.

Racism is perpetuated in *religion* by the misinterpretation of the Word of God in Genesis 9:18–29 by believers on the curse of Canaan (not Ham) as a curse on the black race. When his father, Noah, said, "Cursed be Canaan; a servant of servants he shall be to his brethren." Price et. al (1982) states that there is nothing mentioned about any of Canaan's descendants being cursed. Noah pronounced the curse on his son, not God. God blessed Noah and all three of his sons.[34] Additionally, theologians use Ephesians 5 on master-servant duties and Onesimus in Philemon to justify slavery. Regardless to the excuse used, slavery is not in line with the character of God. Humanity has failed to honor what God has entrusted into his hands and have abused that trust.

Racism engrained itself into the hearts of not only the white people who abused its power, but the African Americans upon whom it was subjected. Thus, the abolition of slavery, while aiding in the betterment of *African American education*, could not cease to rid of the racial gap due to the continued existence of racism within the American people (Bertocchi, 2012).

---

[34] Frederick K. C. Price, *The Truth About… Race: Did God Curse Black People?* (Los Angeles: Faith One Publishing, 1982).

The concept of "Fake News" is not a new term for the African American. Our history books, news reports are filled with untruths, half-truths, and simply blatant lies. A report's perspective is tainted by individual world views and personal bias. If a reporter's perception of an African American is already negative, they will seek and report the negative, while hiding the same flaws in another race.

Every sphere of society is impacted by racism, even the sphere of celebration. While African Americans are more likely to play sports, entertain, and participate in the arts, the roles in entertainment still reflect societies views of African Americans. Sports appear to be the major vehicle for the African American in American society.

Many people attempted to use the Bible to justify the institution of slavery. They make mention that Abraham had slaves and that Apostle Paul returned the slave Onesimus back to his master Philemon to be received as a brother, not a slave. What they fail to reveal is that Hebrew slaves were not assigned to slavery for life. The Hebrew slavery system is described in Deuteronomy 15:12–18:

> If your brother, a Hebrew man or a Hebrew woman, *is sold to you, he shall serve you six years, and in the seventh year you shall let him go free from you.* And when you let him go free from you, *you shall not let him go empty-handed.* You shall furnish him liberally out of your flock, out of your threshing floor, and out of your winepress. As the LORD your God has blessed you, you shall give to him. You shall remember that you were a slave in the land of Egypt, and the LORD your God redeemed you; therefore I command you this today. But if he says to you, "I will not go out from you," because he loves you and your household, since he is well-off with you, then you shall take an awl, and put it through his ear into the door, and he shall be your slave forever. And to your female slave you shall do the same. It shall not seem hard to you when you let him go free

from you, for at half the cost of a hired worker he
has served you six years. So, the LORD your God
will bless you in all that you do.

I am appalled at Christian people who use God's word to justify such a horrible institution as slavery. There is nothing about slavery that reflects the love of God.

Social conditions in contemporary America still reflect a "problem of the color line." The dream that race might someday become an insignificant category in our civic life now seems naively utopian. In cities across the country, and in rural areas of the Old South, the situation of the black underclass and, increasingly, of the black lower working classes is bad and getting worse. No well-informed person denies this, though there is debate over what can and should be done about it. Nor do serious people deny that the crime, drug addiction, family breakdown, unemployment, poor school performance, welfare dependency, and general decay in these communities constitute a blight on our society virtually unrivaled in scale and severity by anything to be found elsewhere in the industrial West. What is sometimes denied, but what must be recognized, is that this is, indeed, a race problem. In a word, they suffer a pariah status. It should not require enormous powers of perception to see how this degradation relates to the shameful history of black-white race relations in this country.[35]

Despite the laws that were enacted because of the civil rights movement and the brave men and women that gave their lives for changes to occur, the laws did not change the hearts of men. Therefore, the laws only provided enslavement in another wrapper, as the laws allowed the sheets of the Klu Klux Klan to be removed, and replaced with judges' robes and attorneys' suits, hiding behind masks in the criminal justice system. Credit scores derived from discriminatory practices that forces higher interest rates hiding behind masks in the economic system. Educational inequities, stereotyping, profil-

---

[35.] Glenn C. Loury, "An American Tragedy: The Legacy of Slavery Lingers in Our Cities' Ghettos," The Brookings Institution (1998).

ing, false incarcerations, police brutality, and legal murders replacing lynchings of earlier years. Just as Jim Crow Laws were enacted to further segregation, unenforced laws make the racial divide continue, only wrapped in a different cover.

Make no mistake, there are decent men and women of all races. However, in each of our systems, there remain those who hide behind a mask and use their influence to infiltrate society, just as the Willie Lynch letter of 1712 on how to make a slave stated, "I have a foolproof method for controlling your black slaves. I guarantee every one of you that if installed correctly it will control the slaves for at least 300 years."[36]

Guilty as charged, but no need for condemnation, just repentance. Time to take all masks off and get rid of the slave mentality. Racism is a learned behavior. This means that children are taught to be racist, prejudiced. Whatever the reason for hating your brother, one thing is for certain, it is not from God.

> If a man say, I love God, and hateth his brother, he is a liar: for he that loveth not his brother whom he hath seen, how can he love God whom he hath not seen? And this commandment have we from him, That he who loveth God love his brother also. (1 John 4:20–21, KJV)

Even today, there remains many wounded hearts infected and inflicted by the sin of racism, discrimination and color bias. Wounds that can only be healed when hearts are yielded and ready to receive true healing from the inside out, not another Band-Aid by unrepentant apologies. Unity is especially important when we are unified for a cause that is not detrimental to ourselves and others.

Consider the story of the Tower of Babel in Genesis 11:1, 4, and 9:

[36.] "The Willie Lynch Letter: The Making Of A Slave!" https://archive.org/stream/WillieLynchLetter1712/the_willie_lynch_letter_the_making_of_a_slave_1712_djvu.txt

> And the whole earth was of one language, and of one speech. And they said, Go to, let us build us a city and a tower, whose top *may reach* unto heaven; *and let us make us a name*, lest we be scattered abroad upon the face of the whole earth. Therefore, is the name of it called Babel; because the LORD did there confound the language of all the earth: and from thence did the LORD scatter them abroad upon the face of all the earth.

It is apparent that God had created man so that they could do anything when they were unified. Unfortunately, as it is today, the people were only interested in themselves. If they were in unity and understood one another, they could build a city that would go up to heaven that *they* could be exalted. God confounded the languages at this point so that they could not understand one another and scattered them across the land.

Similarly, our history is filled with instances in which we unify for the wrong reason, and other instances where we unify for the good of all people. White slave holders unified to continue slavery, white supremists unified to declare the white race superior, Civil Rights activists (both white and black) unified for the rights of all people, and Black Lives Matter groups unified to declare that black lives matter also. In each of these instances, men did what was right in their own eyes. Some with evil motives, others seeking change. Despite the separation of decades between the Civil Rights movement and the problems of today, Bishop Charles Blake states, "I see similarities in the cries for justice against police brutality. What is obviously different today is this: the civil rights movement was visibly God-centric in its motivational speeches, there were many calls for prayer and appeals to the biblical justification of the movement."[37]

---

[37] Bishop Charles Blake, "God's Place in Black History," Christianity Today (2016), https://www.christianitytoday.com/ct/2016/february-web-only/gods-place-in-black-history.html.

Unifying to bring about healing for all races starts with admitting that a problem has and continues to exist, being willing to repent, forgive, and allow God to transform our hearts with the truth of his word, by everyone choosing to change. It is also important that we no longer teach these toxic values to future generations. Hatred taught or seen in the home manifests itself in society in the form of bullying, bombings, shootings, discrimination, unjust treatment, police brutality, distrust of authority, color bias, bigotry, etc. If we want to see the nation healed, we must start with "self." To thine own self be true. Then we can become infectious with the love of God, instead of the toxic hatred that is evident in our culture.

We are not responsible for another man's actions, but we are responsible for our actions and our response. Healing must start somewhere, as painful as it is to continuously fight racism and color bias, it is a natural existence built into our system of government by people who made laws that furthered their interest at the expense of another human being. However, I have noticed over the years that for all of those who are influenced by powers of darkness, God has strategically placed people of all races to take a stand for what He proposes in his word. "Then Peter opened *his* mouth, and said, Of a truth I perceive that God is no respecter of persons: But in every nation he that feareth him, and worketh righteousness, is accepted with him" (Acts 10:34–35, KJV). It is not God that divides along racial lines, but man (in his selfishness).

Unfortunately, without the wisdom of God and the love of God guiding our lives, the USA and the world at large has become prey for the enemy, as he continues to divide and conquer. "And Jesus knew their thoughts, and said unto them, 'Every kingdom divided against itself is brought to desolation; and every city or house divided against itself shall not stand'" (Matthew 12:25, KJV). It is evident from our history, that there has been division over the concept of slavery and the right of a people to be valued, respected, and free since the inception of these United States of America. The time for repentance, healing, and a spiritual revolution is now.

SECTION 4

Sound the Alarm

Nation Under Siege

Call to Me and I will answer you and tell you [and
even show you] great and mighty things, [things which
have been confined and hidden], which you do not
know *and* understand *and* cannot distinguish.

—Jeremiah 33:3 (AMP)

An alarm is going out throughout the earth, summoning the people of God to take their rightful place in society, in the authority of Jesus Christ. We are numerous in number, yet our impact on culture and the world seems to have weakened. When we look at the gospels and Jesus's ministry, He and his disciples made such an impact on their world that it still resonates two thousand years later. Jesus said that we would do greater works than what He had done. Jesus finished his work of redemption; however, He left us to spread the Good News that man can be reconciled back to God. He provided the way, but the ministry of reconciliation rests in our hands.

Ministry of reconciliation is not just preaching that Jesus has paid the price for our redemption, and we can choose Him as our Savior and be reconciled back to God, but we must work on reconciliation among ourselves. Racism does not, in any sense of the word, look like Jesus or resemble his ways and actions. It was God who said that He was no respecter of persons. Yet, our pride has allowed us over the centuries to hold onto old traditions, old wounds handed down generation after generation.

Know this, there is no way that you can wrong your brother and not be seen by God. It is not Russia or terrorism from outside that we should fear, but the deceptive tactics that have infiltrated our nation from its inception of the wrongs done to one another, especially among believers.

I remember becoming tired of praying about injustice and racism prior to 2012, and I was openly rebuked by God because I finally spoke the words, "It has been this way since I was born, and it will always be this way." Immediately in my spirit, I sensed the Holy Spirit correcting me. Somewhere on the inside of me I heard these words: "So you're saying racism is too hard for me?"

"No God," I said aloud. "I just meant it didn't seem that you cared about it." He then reminded me of Luke 1:37: "For with God *nothing* [*is* or ever] shall be *impossible*," and Mark 10:27: "With people [as far as it depends on them] it is impossible, but not with God; for all things are possible with God."

As I repented of my unbelief, I had to ask God to give me grace to believe something that I had cried out to Him since I was ten years of age, in 1965. Now, forty-seven years later, with daily confrontations of racism and institutional racism, I felt tired of praying. This is when He reminded me of Jeremiah 33:3 (my personal word from the Lord), which has sustained me when nothing seems to go right. I know that I can call on Him and He will answer me and show me supernatural things that only He can do.

At that time, I received one statement from God, that this book has sought to explore: "It cannot be accomplished by the marches of the 1960's, but by a spiritual revolution." These were God's words to me in 2012. With these words came Jeremiah 32:17: "Ah Lord God! behold, thou hast made the heaven and the earth by thy great power and stretched out arm, and there is *nothing too hard* for thee," and Jeremiah 32:27: "Behold, I am the Lord, the God of all flesh: is there anything *too hard* for me?" I knew in my heart that although God had spared me from the atrocities that my ancestors faced of slavery, the effects of slavery had lingered for generations among whites and blacks.

The most appalling of all things was that this division was promoted, and many times started by Christians. But the alarm was now sounding loud. Even as God told Cain (after he murdered his brother) that your brother's blood cries out from the ground. So, too,

I hear the Lord in his compassion speaking to the Body of Christ again.

> If my people, who are called by my name, will humble themselves and pray and seek my face and turn from their wicked ways, then I will hear from heaven, and I will forgive their sin and will heal their land. (2 Chronicles 7:14)

America is at war, not with Russia, but with itself. She refuses to honor what God honors and submit to God rather than to tradition, culture, and our own way. God does not force Himself on anyone, and He extends mercy before judgment. However, though the sin nature has been taken care of for the believer, it is our responsibility to renew our minds daily with the word of God, choose God's way above our ancestors' way, and present our bodies (black and white) as living sacrifices before God.

The world will never see Jesus through the double standards of division that remains in the church. Yet, God is never without a people who will relinquish their will and obey the will of God. That is the company of believers for which I associate myself. As painful as racism is, "Child of God," we must take the masks off and be open before God. I had to ask Him to help me forgive. Amazingly, He softened my heart while writing this book; and while I have a long way to go, I believe that as I continue to submit to God and resist the deception of satan, I will be a true imitator of God.

Hiding Behind the Mask

But mark this: There will be terrible times in the last days. People
will be lovers of themselves, lovers of money, boastful, proud,
abusive, disobedient to their parents, ungrateful, unholy, without
love, unforgiving, slanderous, without self-control, brutal,
not lovers of the good, treacherous, rash, conceited, lovers of
pleasure rather than lovers of God—having a form of godliness
but denying its power. Have nothing to do with such people.

—2 Timothy 3:1–5 (NIV)

Taking a deep look into the mirror shows our outward appearance,
but the truth of God's word can expose the heart. Unfortunately,
God's word has been misused for man's convenience rather than for
heart transformation. This has caused many in the Body of Christ to
appear hypocritical.

God chose to use mankind to accomplish his plan in the earth;
however, mankind abused what God had entrusted to him. It took
me a long time to understand the satanic contradictions of my reality
and the truth of God's word about me. Now, I understand that all
races have been cheated by allowing division to keep us from receiv-
ing God's best for our lives. We need one another. James 3:16 says,
"For where envying and strife is, there is confusion and *every evil
work.*" Selfishness has plagued our nation and society. While there
appears to be little or no hope, we know that God always causes us to
triumph in Christ Jesus.

Humbling ourselves before God will cause us to take a good
look at ourselves considering God's word. We spend much time fix-
ing the outside but little time in God's word, which is the only way

we can renew our minds with his way of doing things. I constantly go to God's word for direction, for He has instructed us to trust Him with our heart and lean not to our understanding, but to acknowledge Him, and He would direct our path.

I especially needed his direction trying to understand why the KKK was so prevalent in a Christian society, or why they hid behind sheets, only to find out that some of these people were "Christians." When I began to understand that man is a three-part being and only his spirit is recreated at the new birth, but his mind had to be renewed with God's word for his heart to be transformed then I understood how this could be possible. I then understood the need for the sheet. Even as Adam hid himself with fig leaves in the garden because he knew he was wrong, so too the inner man alerts us when we are doing wrong; however, we have the choice to be led by the Spirit of God or yield to our emotions (a part of our soul). Also, our human spirit is only in alignment with the Holy Spirit to the degree that we feed our spirit with his word, to get his mind (a part of our soul) renewed. James 1:21 says, "Wherefore lay apart all filthiness and superfluity of naughtiness, and receive with meekness the engrafted word, which is able to save your souls."

I now understand the need to hide when our conscious conflicts with our actions. Injustice has been masked within the laws of our land since its inception when the laws are enforced to only protect the majority. I caution you however, as you hide behind your masks, that God still sees everything and everyone. Although He is merciful, full of grace, compassionate, and loving, He is also a just God (even to people of color).

So, judges, when you intentionally give harsher sentences based upon race, or attorneys who automatically assume guilt for people of color and allow innocent people to be incarcerated, you are hiding behind a mask. Police officers that abuse their authority, plant evidence, withhold evidence, falsify reports, and murder innocent people, you are hiding behind a mask. People of color who commit crimes against others out of self-hatred, hopelessness, and an unrecognized agreement with society that certain lives are less valuable than other lives, you are hiding behind a mask. Ministers of the Gospel that have used God's word to manipulate and control based upon personal bias, you are hiding behind a mask, Media and entertainment that stereotype in casting characters, or falsifying information based upon personal bias, you are hiding behind a mask. White Americans that hate blacks because they were taught to hate or learned hatred, you are without excuse; you are hiding behind a mask. God entrusted this land to mankind (all men), but you have abused his gift. You must repent instead of hiding behind a mask. He gave mankind (all races) dominion over the earth, not over one another. Black Americans that assume that all whites are evil because you were taught to mistrust, and even learned to mistrust; you must learn to forgive and not continue to hide behind the mask. For every person that has allowed their personal bias to cause harm to another, let's take the masks off and repent before God. We cannot accomplish a heart change on our own, but when we are willing to allow God, He will give us grace to love one another and honor one another for who He created us to be.

I cannot hide behind the masks that society has given me because of labels that have been assigned me. When I walk into a store and know that I am being trailed, I cannot allow their ignorance to cause anger and bitterness in me. I must recognize and know who the real enemy is.

Knowing the Enemy

In conclusion, be strong in the Lord [draw your strength from Him and be empowered through your union with Him] and in the power of His [boundless] might. Put on the full armor of God [for His precepts are like the splendid armor of a heavily-armed soldier], so that you may be able to [successfully] stand up against all the schemes *and* the strategies *and* the deceits of the devil. *For our struggle is not against flesh and blood* [contending only with physical opponents], but against the rulers, against the powers, against the world forces of this [present] darkness, against the spiritual *forces* of wickedness in the heavenly (supernatural) *places.*

—Ephesians 6:10–12 (AMP)

As the Body of Christ, we should know by now that we should not be fighting one another, but we should be so focused on God that we readily discern who is responsible for division, confusion, hatred, and any form of disobedience. We have the truth about how to treat one another. Jesus is the fulfillment of the law, and God is love. If God is love, and He has shed his love in our heart after the Holy Ghost, we must simply choose whether to yield to our spirit or our flesh. Jesus said in John 14:9, "Have I been so long time with you, and yet hast thou not known me, Philip? he that hath seen me hath seen the Father; and how sayest thou *then*, Shew us the Father?" Mark 3:24–25 says, "And if a kingdom be divided against itself, that kingdom cannot stand. And if a house be divided against itself, that house cannot stand."

Deception and division is the method that satan has used throughout history. The disgrace is the Body of Christ falling prey to his schemes. As we attack one another through injustice, unjust weights and balances, false incarcerations, threats and intimidation, bitterness and hatred, our singing about the love of God seems to contradict our actions.

> *There is* therefore now no condemnation to them which are in Christ Jesus, who walk not after the flesh, but after the Spirit. (Romans 8:1, KJV)

Let's wise up, children of God, and fight the right enemy (satan). He has already been defeated by Jesus, but it's up to us to enforce the victory we already have. However, we remain powerless if we continue to play by his rules. Hatred is not part of God's nature. The only thing that He hates is sin, not the sinner. Let's take our focus off ourselves and place our focus on God: his will and his way. Once we saturate ourselves with the truth of his word and his presence, we will begin to see the beauty in the differences that we each bring. No man is superior than another, nor is any man inferior to another. Only man came up with these standards. I choose the standards of God and not the warped opinions of man. Let's not pass the toxic hatred of discrimination and racism to another generation.

Brothers and sisters in the Lord, we are without excuse. We are responsible for the condition of this world. We must be very sure that this Holy Word that we are teaching is rightly divided according to the Spirit of God. We must be sure that our spirit is not yielding to another spirit, other than the Spirit of God.

Healing All Wounds

I have indeed seen the oppression of my people in Egypt.
I have heard their groaning and have come down to set
them free. Now come, I will send you back to Egypt.

—Acts 17:34 (NIV)

One who was there had been an invalid for thirty-eight years. When
Jesus saw him lying there and learned that he had been in this
condition for a long time, he asked him, "Do you want to get well?"

—John 5:5–6 (NIV)

We are a blessed people in that we no longer have shackles around our ankles and our necks as our ancestors had. Unfortunately, those shackles still exist in our minds and on our hearts. In our minds because it is a constant, daily battle to fight against a system that devalues certain people because of the color of their skin. This constant struggle will lead to a slave mentality if left unchecked.

When I hear statements such as "go back where you came from," I'm amazed at the bigotry that still exists in our society. Amazingly, they forget that we are all immigrants, except native Americans. I listen as I hear that blacks consume welfare, and I think of the years that our ancestors made wealth for others and received nothing while they themselves were treated as property. I listen as I hear that our men are raping their women, as I watch white women boast about their ability to take "our" men, and many black men buy the lie that white women are somehow more feminine, more beautiful, more valuable than black women. My heart aches as I think of the women whom God created to love and be loved, but must accept no one rather than be treated as if she is nothing. I weep when I see and hear of another innocent person murdered, with no laws to protect them, only because their skin is darker.

> How God anointed Jesus of Nazareth with the Holy Ghost and with power: who went about doing good and healing all that were *oppressed* of the devil; for God was with him. (Acts 10:38, KJV)

I am so thankful that God has delivered us from the diabolical system of slavery; however, because the laws of the land were made by slave owners, it seems understandable that personal biases were a part of our law. The laws of the land are subjective and take on the values of those creating the law. Yet God has continuously shown Himself strong on our behalf despite all odds.

Acts 17 tells the story of Stephen, a disciple of Jesus Christ, who is about to be stoned for his belief in Jesus Christ. Stephen relays the history of his ancestors and their time in slavery. In the face of death, Stephen still knows that although he is about to die, he remembers that God allowed his ancestors to be oppressed by Pharaoh for years. It was not because he did not love Israel, but his compassion and mercy for all people was giving Pharaoh an opportunity to repent. However, Pharaoh's heart had become hardened, and he refused to let the people go. Despite many warnings, Pharaoh held fast in keeping Israel enslaved. However, there came a time when God delivered his people from the oppression of Pharaoh, and Pharaoh and his entire army were drowned. Because we live in a fallen world, people make choices that impact our lives. However, God is faithful to keep his promise to those who are obedient to Him.

Although it may seem like a long time, God's hand is not shortened that He cannot save. Even with the invalid in John 5; he had been in his condition for thirty-eight years and had lost hope. I can hear Jesus asking him, "Do you want to be well"? It seems like a question that need not be asked; surely a sick person wants to be well. However, we can be in a condition so long that we lose hope of it ever being any other way. But just as Jesus healed the sick man after thirty-eight years, He will heal broken hearts, wounded spirits, and any other oppression that the enemy has placed in our lives. I choose to say as Peter said in Luke 5:5, "And Simon answering said unto him, Master, we have toiled all the night, and have taken nothing: nevertheless, at thy word I will let down the net." Although it seems that I have prayed and prayed with little result, I say like Peter, "Nevertheless at thy word, I will continue to follow and obey you, Lord."

> And *I will restore* to you the years that the locust hath eaten, the cankerworm, and the caterpiller, and the palmerworm, my great army which *I* sent among you. (Joel 2:25, KJV)

We all need the healing power of God to restore us. Many of us are blind, not physically but spiritually blind to what is happening to us and among us. Many of us are wounded and have buried the wounds inside so long that the love of God can't flow through freely. Hurting people, hurt people. There is a desperate need for our nation to be healed. We must pray for one another that we would be healed, and that healing would flow from individuals to families, to cities, to states, to nations, and throughout the world. We must celebrate our differences rather than allowing the enemy to use our differences as a means of division.

SECTION 5

Christianity and Racism

Christian

Then Barnabas went to Tarsus to look for Saul, and when he found him, he brought him to Antioch. So, for a whole year Barnabas and Saul met with the church and taught great numbers of people. The *disciples were called Christians first at Antioch.*

—Acts 11:25–26 (NIV)

Christian, a word formed after the Roman style, signifying an adherent of Jesus, was first applied to such by the Gentiles. In 1 Peter 4:16, the Apostle Peter is speaking from a point of view of the persecutor. Early implications of scorn, but from second century onward, the term was accepted by believers as a title of honor. Webster's dictionary defines Christian as one who professes belief in the teachings of Jesus Christ.

In our American society today, being a Christian has taken on a different meaning than during the time of the disciples. Christian to many mean church attendance or doing good deeds (i.e., being a good person). However, being a good person without accepting Jesus Christ as Lord and Savior still means that you are not saved. We cannot be good enough in our own efforts to satisfy the debt of sin; only Jesus was a perfect man and could offer Himself in our place.

Everything that God did was out of love for us. I love the story about Nicodemus in John 3. He inquired of Jesus what it meant to be born again. He wanted to know how he could reenter his mother's womb and be reborn. This is when Jesus explains to Nicodemus that his first birth was a natural birth (born of the flesh from the seed of a man, from his mother and father). However, the "new birth," "salvation," "born again," "saved," is being born of the Spirit of God by faith in Jesus Christ. Only when we accept Jesus as Savior can we be born again.

> If you declare with your mouth, "Jesus is Lord,"
> and believe in your heart that God raised him from
> the dead, you will be saved. (Romans 10:9, NIV)

Once we accept Jesus as our Lord and Savior, the nature of sin is replaced with the nature of God, and we become a new creation in Christ Jesus. However, only our spirit is recreated. We still must renew our mind (part of our soul) with the word of God, and present our bodies as living sacrifices to God. The more we feed our spirit and are led by the Holy Spirit, the more like Jesus we become. "Therefore, if anyone is in Christ, the new creation has come: The old has gone, the new is here!" (2 Corinthians 5:17).

Therefore, it should not be the nature of a Christian to be prejudiced or racist. God is love. The very nature of God is love, and He has shed that love in our hearts once we are saved. When we are motivated by anything other than love, we are not being led by the Spirit of God but by the flesh. First John 4:20 and 1 Corinthians 13:4-7 tell us how that love should look.

> Whoever claims to love God yet hates *a* brother
> or sister *is a liar.* For whoever does not love their
> brother and sister, whom they have seen, cannot
> love God, whom they have not seen. (1 John
> 4:20, NIV)

> Love endures with patience *and* serenity, love is
> kind *and* thoughtful, and is not jealous *or* envious;
> love does not brag and is not proud *or* arrogant.
> It is not rude; it is not self-seeking, it is not pro-
> voked [nor overly sensitive and easily angered];
> it does not take into account a wrong *endured.* It
> does not rejoice at injustice but rejoices with the
> truth [when right and truth prevail]. Love bears

all things [regardless of what comes], believes all things [looking for the best in each one], hopes all things [remaining steadfast during difficult times], endures all things [without weakening]. (1 Corinthians 13:4–7, AMP)

Racism and prejudice are the result of sin. First John says that we lie when we say we love God but hate our brothers or sisters. If Adam and Eve were the only beings created to populate the earth, Noah and his sons are descendants of Adam and Eve, and every other human on earth must be related in some way. We must repent, forgive, and choose to walk in love with each of our brothers and sisters so that our prayers are not hindered.

Separated Unto God

Teacher, which is the greatest commandment in the Law?" And Jesus replied to him, "'You shall *love the Lord your God* with all your heart, and with all your soul, and with all your mind.' This is the *first and greatest commandment.* The *second* is like it, 'You shall *love your neighbor as yourself [that is, unselfishly seek the best or higher good for others].*' The whole Law and the [writings of the] Prophets depend on these two commandments."

—Matthew 22:36–40 (AMP)

Wherefore come out from among them, and *be ye separate*, saith the Lord, and touch not the unclean thing; and I will receive you.

—2 Corinthians 6:17 (KJV)

Many have interpreted 2 Corinthians 6:17 to mean to physically come out from among unbelievers; however, when we look at Jesus's ministry on earth, we often find Him among sinners. He ate with publicans and tax collectors. While we are not to behave as the world and partake of their methods of living, we are instructed to go into all the world and preach the Gospel. Jesus said in John 6:38, "For I came down from heaven, not to do mine own will, but the will of him that sent me." This should always be our aim, to fulfill the plan of God, acting as his ambassadors in the earth. We are not to think of ourselves better than unbelievers, but our chaste conversation and love for God and others should reflect and imitate the character of God always.

Second Corinthians 6:17, in context, was talking about being unequally yoked with unbelievers. The objective is to be separated unto God in such a way that unbelievers can see Jesus in us always. It is not a forced performance but what flows from within because of the time that we spend in fellowship with our father God. This is not just physically; even our conversation and lifestyle should reflect Jesus, and not the world. Most people can agree with adultery, fornication, stealing, etc. as sin, but we ignore hatred by racism as if it is one of those things that can be tolerated as something other than sin.

We have used the word "love" so loosely in our society that many don't know what God's definition of love is. First Corinthians reminds us that it does not matter how many times you prophesy and speak in tongues; if you don't have love for your fellow man (including unbelievers), your words will fall on deaf ears. We, as the Body of Christ, must set the example for the world. This may be uncomfortable to our flesh; however, if we are interested in doing things God's way and not our own, we will obey God and separate ourselves unto his will, his plan, his purpose, and his way of living. Matthew Henry Commentary Online expresses it this way: "Come out from the workers of iniquity and separate from their vain and sinful pleasures and pursuits; from all conformity to the corruptions of this present evil world. If it be an envied privilege to be the son or daughter of an earthly prince, who can express the dignity and happiness of being sons and daughters of the Almighty?"

Even as Isaiah 52 talks about Jerusalem being delivered from Babylonian captivity, it is also reminding the priests and Levites and all Jerusalem to bring no polluted things of Babylon with them, as Israel had done when they came out of Egypt. The customs and rituals of Egypt were brought into the culture of Israel. To avoid this happening again, Jerusalem has clear instructions from God. We too must love all people; however, the Christian has become too much like the world, instead of our being an influence on the world. Every decision that we make, every way that we live, must be as unto the Lord in both our private and public lives.

Separated unto God in every area of our lives means that within every sphere of influence within society, God has strategically placed his people. However, we must be separated unto Him, so that his Spirit is what flows out of us because his word is what we have been putting within us.

Ministry of Reconciliation

For we [believers will be called to account and] must all appear before the judgment seat of Christ, so that each one may be repaid for what has been done in the body, whether good or bad [that is, each will be held responsible for his actions, purposes, goals, motives—the use or misuse of his time, opportunities and abilities].

—2 Corinthians 5:10 (AMP)

So, from now on we regard no one from a worldly point of view. Though we once regarded Christ in this way, we do so no longer. Therefore, *if anyone is in Christ, the new creation has come: The old has gone, the new is here! All this is from God, who reconciled us to himself through Christ and gave us the ministry of reconciliation*: that God was reconciling the world to himself in Christ, not counting people's sins against them. And he has committed to us the message of reconciliation.

—2 Corinthians 5:16–19 (NIV)

As believers, we have been given the privilege to share the Gospel (good news) with the world. This sharing of the Gospel is the message of reconciliation, that God has reconciled the world to Himself through Christ Jesus, not counting man's sins against them. This is for anyone who will accept Jesus as Savior and Lord of their lives. He paid the price for the sins of the world so that our spirit can once again have the nature of God, instead of the evil, sinful nature of satan. So, although the sin nature is paid for and we are no longer a slave to sin because we have the nature of Christ, we can still choose to disobey and ignore the Spirit of God.

An unbeliever will be judged because he refused Jesus and will be judged based upon his own works since he has not accepted the finished works of Jesus; however, the believer is redeemed because Jesus paid the penalty for the sin nature, and we stand in righteousness through Jesus Christ. We, however, will give an account for those things that we did in the body, not the spirit. We will be repaid or rewarded for things we did, whether good or bad.

> For everything in the world—the lust of the flesh, the lust of the eyes, and the pride of life—comes not from the Father but from the world. (1 John 2:16, NIV)

Believers, let's choose to submit to the Spirit of God instead of the world system. Let us choose to do things God's way, so when we share the good news, it comes from our heart and not our head. Let us turn the nation around beginning within us, our families, our nation, and our world. This can only be done by allowing God to circumcise our hearts. He won't force his way in; He must be invited. God's word says that there is nothing too hard for Him—not even racism. However, it's all a choice for everyone, individually.

> This day I call the heavens and the earth as witnesses against you that I have set before you life and death, blessings and curses. Now choose life, so that you and your children may live. (Deuteronomy 30:19, NIV)

The more we know who we are, what we have, and the authority that we have as believers, the more equipped we will be to stand in that authority against the tricks of satan. The signs and wonders that follow the word was for the unbeliever to see the manifestation of God. Believers are to live by faith in the word of God every day, knowing that He always causes us to triumph in Christ Jesus. Then our message that Jesus reconciled the world back to God will have merit, and the world will have a reason to believe that there is something different about the people of God.

"In Christ" Realities

Therefore, if anyone is in Christ, he is a new creation; old things have passed away; behold, all things have become new.

—2 Corinthians 5:17 (NKJV)

For in Christ the fullness of God lives in a human body, and you are complete through your union with Christ. He is the Lord over every ruler and authority in the universe.

—Colossians 2:9–10 (NLT)

Once we know who we are in Jesus Christ as believers, then we will begin to act like our Father. We cannot imitate that which we do not know about. That is why we must decide to submit to God, study his word, get in his presence, pray in the Spirit, and allow the Holy Spirit to transform our hearts and minds to be and think like Christ.

The term "creation" in Webster's dictionary is defined as "a complete new species of being which never before existed." This is exactly what we become when we are born again, "a complete new species of being which never before existed." Our identity with Jesus Christ is the most life-changing truth the believer can ever come to realize and walk in. All that we will ever become or accomplish for the kingdom of God is dependent upon our realization of our identity with Jesus Christ.

Psychologists have asserted that as we grow, we develop our self-concept through identification with others. This involves the incorporation of the characteristics of our parents and other adults by adopting their appearance, attitudes, and behaviors. Children will naturally tend to identify with those persons to whom they are emotionally attached. When our sense of identity is determined by any other person, activity, or object other than what God determines, we can fall prey to every sort of deception and destructive behavior. If the believer allows the world around them to dictate their identity, they will remain bound by the carnal nature.[38]

Below is a chart of some of our "In Christ" realities that every believer must come to know.

"In Christ" Realities	
Scripture (NIV)	Verse
I am a child of God Romans 8:16	The Spirit himself testifies with our spirit that we are God's children.
I am redeemed from the hand of the enemy Psalms 107:2	Let the redeemed of the LORD tell their story—those he redeemed from the hand of the foe
I am forgiven Colossians 1:13–14	For he has rescued us from the dominion of darkness and brought us into the kingdom of the Son he loves, in whom we have redemption, the forgiveness of sins.
I am saved by grace through faith Ephesians 2:8	For it is by grace you have been saved, through faith—and this is not from yourselves, it is the gift of God
I am a new creature 2 Corinthians 5:17	Therefore, if anyone is in Christ, the new creation has come: The old has gone, the new is here!
I am a partaker of his divine nature 2 Peter 1:4	Through these he has given us his very great and precious promises, so that through them you may participate in the divine nature, having escaped the corruption in the world caused by evil desires.
I am redeemed from the curse of the law Galatians 3:13	Christ redeemed us from the curse of the law by becoming a curse for us, for it is written: "Cursed is everyone who is hung on a pole."
I am delivered from the powers of darkness Colossians 1:13–14	For he has rescued us from the dominion of darkness and brought us into the kingdom of the Son he loves, in whom we have redemption, the forgiveness of sins.

---

38. Timothy Jerry, "Our Identity in Christ," Living Faith Church (2016), https://www.livingfaithchurchwi.org/sermons/our-identity-in-christ/.

I am led by the Spirit of God Romans 8:14	For those who are led by the Spirit of God are the children of God.
I am kept in safety wherever I go Psalms 91:11–12	For he will command his angels concerning you to guard you in all your ways; they will lift you up in their hands, so that you will not strike your foot against a stone.
I am getting all my needs met by Jesus Philippians 4:19	And my God will meet all your needs according to the riches of his glory in Christ Jesus.
I am casting my cares on Jesus 1 Peter 5:7	Cast all your anxiety on him because he cares for you.
I am strong in the Lord and in the power of His might Ephesians 6:10–11	Finally, be strong in the Lord and in his mighty power. Put on the full armor of God, so that you can take your stand against the devil's schemes.
I am doing all things through Christ who strengthens me Philippians 4:13	I can do all this through him who gives me strength.
I am an heir of God and a joint heir with Jesus Romans 8:17	Now if we are children, then we are heirs—heirs of God and co-heirs with Christ, if indeed we share in his sufferings in order that we may also share in his glory.
I am an heir to the blessings of Abraham Galatians 3:13–14	Christ redeemed us from the curse of the law by becoming a curse for us, for it is written: "Cursed is everyone who is hung on a pole." He redeemed us in order that the blessing given to Abraham might come to the Gentiles through Christ Jesus, so that by faith we might receive the promise of the Spirit.
I am blessed coming in and going out, and above only, not beneath Deuteronomy 28:6, 13	You will be blessed when you come in and blessed when you go out. The Lord will make you the head, not the tail. If you pay attention to the commands of the Lord your God that I give you this day and carefully follow them, you will always be at the top, never at the bottom.
I am blessed with all spiritual blessings Ephesians 1:3	Praise be to the God and Father of our Lord Jesus Christ, who has blessed us in the heavenly realms with every spiritual blessing in Christ.
I am an inheritor of eternal life 1 John 5:11–12	And this is the testimony: God has given us eternal life, and this life is in his Son. Whoever has the Son has life; whoever does not have the Son of God does not have life.

I am healed by his stripes 1 Peter 2:24	"He himself bore our sins" in his body on the cross, so that we might die to sins and live for righteousness; "by his wounds you have been healed."
I am exercising my authority over the enemy Luke 10:19	I have given you authority to trample on snakes and scorpions and to overcome all the power of the enemy; nothing will harm you.
I am more than a conqueror Romans 8:37	No, in all these things we are more than conquerors through him who loved us.
I am being transformed by the renewing of my mind Romans 12:2	Do not conform to the pattern of this world, but be transformed by the renewing of your mind. Then you will be able to test and approve what God's will is—his good, pleasing and perfect will.
I am a laborer together with God 1 Corinthians 3:9	For we are co-workers in God's service; you are God's field, God's building.
I am the righteousness of God in Christ 2 Corinthians 5:21	God made him who had no sin to be sin for us, so that in him we might become the righteousness of God.
I am an imitator of Jesus Ephesians 5:1	Follow God's example, therefore, as dearly loved children

SECTION 6

Spiritual Revolution

Spiritual Revolution

The Spirit of the Lord is on me, because he has anointed me to
proclaim good news to the poor. He has sent me to proclaim
freedom for the prisoners and recovery of sight for the blind, to
set the oppressed free, to proclaim the year of the Lord's favor.

—Luke 4:18–19 (NIV)

As I started on this journey, I was distressed because my reality was
contrary to what God's word said to me about my life. From childhood, I watched in sorrow the difference between treatment of white
Americans and black Americans. I had prayed about this situation
from age ten in 1965 when I saw firemen spray blacks with fire hoses
and policemen releasing vicious dogs on them. Despite my tears and
prayers, it seemed that God was silent until 2012 when He gave me
only one statement: "It cannot be accomplished by the marches of
the 1960s, but by a spiritual revolution."

From that day until today, I have been researching our history and the Word of God to make some sense of my existence in
a world where God says that I have spiritual authority. Revolution
has many meanings. However, we are only interested in a spiritual
revolution. Dictionary.com defines revolution as a sudden, complete,
or marked change in something. Webster's dictionary defines it as a
sudden, radical, or complete change. A fundamental change in the
way of thinking about or visualizing something: a change of para-
digm. Vines Expository Dictionary defines spiritual as things that
have their origin with God, and which, therefore, are in harmony
with his character.

> We can make our own plans, but the LORD GIVES
> THE RIGHT ANSWER. (PROVERBS 16:1, NLT)

As I researched the meaning of spiritual revolution, I found a consensus among believers and unbelievers alike. In an article by KOJC (Kingdom of Jesus Christ), it was stated that Jesus Christ authored the spiritual revolution (a revolution that changed man's heart). He was considered the greatest revolutionary that ever lived. He walked the earth obeying the will of his Father. He and his disciples turned the world around with his preaching, teaching, delivering, and loving the people. A spiritual revolution takes place when one decides by his own freedom of choice to follow the life of absolute obedience to God through his Son, Jesus Christ. This is totally contrary to doing your own human will. When you follow God, you surrender to the ways of the Son of God.[39]

Jesus himself said that the greatest commandment is love. This means to love God first with all our heart, mind, and strength and to love our neighbor as ourselves. Based upon the treatment of mankind to one another, I wonder if we love ourselves, or are we ignorant to what love actually is from God's perspective.

> Love endures with patience *and* serenity, love is
> kind *and* thoughtful, and is not jealous *or* envious;
> love does not brag and is not proud *or* arrogant.
> It is not rude; it is not self-seeking, it is not pro-
> voked [nor overly sensitive and easily angered];
> it does not take into account a wrong *endured*. It
> does not rejoice at injustice but rejoices with the
> truth [when right and truth prevail]. Love bears
> all things [regardless of what comes], believes all
> things [looking for the best in each one], hopes
> all things [remaining steadfast during difficult

---

[39] KOJC Admin, "The Spiritual Revolution," The Kingdom of Jesus Christ (2014), https://kingdomofjesuschrist.org/the-spiritual-revolution/.

times], endures all things [without weakening].
(1 Corinthians 13:4–7, AMP)

If anyone says, "I *love* God," and hates (works against) his [Christian] brother he *is a liar*; for the one who *does not love* his brother whom he has seen, cannot *love* God whom he has *not* seen.
(1 John 4:20, AMP)

Truly loving someone means seeking the best for them. Oppression is never the best for any man. In an article on spiritual revolution, Matthew Fox states, "Fear is the door in the heart that lets evil spirits in." Fox further states that a spiritual revolution is a revolution in values and moral protest.[40] Dr. Martin Luther King and his team during the Civil Rights Movement impacted the world by standing against evil in a non-violent way. This group of people courageously fought against injustice, simply protesting oppression based upon race.

In an article by Jennifer LeClaire on February 6, 2018, I was fascinated to see how the Holy Spirit works. While I had my own views on what God meant by spiritual revolution, I was still examining my own heart to ensure that I was getting God's heart on the matter and not my opinion. As I read LeClaire's article, I knew that God had instructed me about a spiritual revolution for me, the Body of Christ, the nation, and the world.

LeClaire says she heard the Holy Spirit say one word: "revolution." She received confirmation from an article in a flight magazine by Matt Phillips called "New Tricks." The Holy Spirit (she says) illuminated the words "There has to be a revolution," says John Belsham. Amazingly, Belsham was a winemaker, and wine is symbolic of the Holy Spirit. An excerpt of the prophecy that was given is below:

---

[40] Matthew Fox, "A (Spiritual) Revolution on the Way," HuffPost, https://m.huffpost.com/us/entry/12991444.

I will move and you will see Me move in extraordinary and unusual ways. But it's not going to look like what you think. So, don't reject what I do, the new wine that I'm pouring out. But prepare your heart even now to receive it. As you read through the gospels and you read the miracles of Jesus, I'm going to give you new revelations, new insight, a new perspective on that what you have read many, many times before because I've called you as change agents in your nation. I've called you, yes, as revival carriers, as kingdom releasers, as glory dwellers in your nation, and I will send you to and fro, not just with the word, but a demonstration of My Spirit. The knowledge of the glory of the Lord will come from this nation.[41]

LeClaire mentions that the Lord wants to bring a new voice of healing movement to New Zealand. During the meeting, she held altar calls for intercessors, millennials, and prophets. God poured out new wine, and there was fire, glory, power, and holy laughter released confirming the word. Although this prophecy was for New Zealand, it is also what I hear God saying for the United States of America.

Stumbling upon this article only confirmed what God said to me in 2012 about a spiritual revolution. While He has not unfolded the whole picture of how the revolution will look and how it will be done, I know that the hearts of man changing is one of the primary outcomes. The laws of the 1960s did not change the hearts of men; they only provided rules for how things should have been. However, when the hearts are not changed, rules are not followed nor enforced. Until the hearts of men change, the deliverance cycle is not complete.

---

[41] Jennifer LeClaire, "Prophecy: God's Heart Is Spiritual Revolution for New Zealand," Charisma Magazine (2018), https://www.charismamag.com/blogs/prophetic-insight/35717-prophecy-god-s-heart-is-spiritual-revolution-for-new-zealand.

Now is the time for each of us to reexamine ourselves and ensure that we have not manipulated God's word for our convenience, traditions, opinions, and biases. When hearts are changed, our land can experience the healing flow of God in every arena of life, not just racism.

> Create in me a clean heart, O God, and renew a right *and* steadfast spirit within me. (Psalm 51:10, AMP)

> All the ways of a man are clean *and* innocent in his own eyes [and he may see nothing wrong with his actions], But the Lord weighs and examines the motives *and* intents [of the heart and knows the truth]. Commit your works to the LORD [SUBMIT AND TRUST THEM TO HIM],

> And your plans will succeed [if you respond to His will and guidance]. (Proverbs 16:2–3, AMP)

For the purposes of this book, it appears the Holy Spirit is sending messages to us of our role in the coming spiritual revolution. Read each message prayerfully with an open heart. Keep in mind that God is love. His instructions to us are out of his love for us. He knows that our disobedience will lead to destruction, but obedience to Him and his word leads to a fulfilled life.

Message to Spiritually Mature Christians

Listen carefully: I have given you authority [that you now possess] to tread on serpents and scorpions, and [the ability to exercise authority] over all the power of the enemy (satan); and nothing will [in any way] harm you.

—Luke 10:19 (AMP)

Come before me and receive clarity for this hour. You stand in authority to turn this nation around; however, I operate through and by love. You must first present yourself before me. You know me, and are known by me, yet you have allowed the distractions of the world to pull you from your first love. I am the essence of life. Everything that you have been seeking already belongs to you. While you are seeking things, I have something far greater than you can imagine.

Many of you have remained silent, although you knew that I was not pleased with what was happening among you. Yet others spoke boldly, but I told you how to speak my truth. "But *speaking* the *truth* in love [in all things—both our speech and our lives expressing His *truth*], let us grow up in all *things* into Him [following His example] who is the Head—Christ" (Ephesians 4:15, AMP). My Body (the Church) must be in unity and walk in love for the nation to take heed. The world cannot see me because many in my body behave like the world. Yes, my grace has been given, but my word clearly says in John 13:34–35, "By this everyone will know that you are my disciples, if you *love one another*." A spiritual revolution comes with your returning to your first love. Seek my face for directions in all matters of life. Don't allow ancestral spirits to entrap you. You stand in authority over the works of the enemy, yet your heart must be pure in order for you to hear me with clarity.

> If the *foundations* [of a godly society] are *destroyed,*
> What can the righteous do? (Psalm 11:3, AMP)

You must privately enter a season of consecration unto me. Spend time in my word, praising me, worshipping me, praying in the spirit; for I have much that I need to have done. It must be done quickly, for I have lingered waiting for you to recognize me and repent of lukewarmness. I have chosen to use you.

I am Good News to all men. Don't allow pride and the sins of generations past to block the flow of my spirit. I call you to love and forgive. Not as the world does, but you know my word. My love has been shed abroad in your heart after the Holy Ghost, so you are without excuse. Now spend time in my presence and your heart will change.

Wouldn't it be shameful if you did all of your religious service here on earth only to hear me say, "Depart from me, I know you not"? I want your heart. When you give me your heart and renew your mind with my word, your behavior will be more in line with who I am. You already have been given this spirit; now walk in it.

You cannot do this on your own. This is where you have failed. I left you a good example. I even came to live in you. You have accepted me as your Savior; now allow me to be your Lord. The choice is yours. I have not changed my plan for you from the foundation of the world. You decide the harvest that you will reap by what you choose to sow. I have given you the grace; now you must choose to allow me to change your heart. It is growing, maturing in me. I await only you. I need you as a watchman on the wall for the nation, but first you must be ready lest the evil one influence you also.

Message to Carnal (Immature) Christians

Therefore I urge you, brothers and sisters, by the mercies of God, to *present your bodies* [dedicating all of yourselves, set apart] as a living sacrifice, holy and well-pleasing to God, *which is* your rational (logical, intelligent) act of worship. And do not be conformed to this world [any longer with its superficial values and customs], but *be transformed and* progressively changed [as you mature spiritually] *by the renewing of your mind* [focusing on godly values and ethical attitudes], so that you may prove [for yourselves] what the will of God is, that which is good and acceptable and perfect [in His plan and purpose for you].

—Romans 12:1–2 (AMP)

I love you, my child, but you must grow up in me. You have accepted me as your Savior, but I am not your Lord. I want to be your Lord and Savior. You have chosen your traditions, your will, your opinion, your race over and above my word. When you accepted me as your Savior, your spirit was recreated, so you have everything within you that you need to mature in me. However, just as you had to choose me as Savior, you must choose me as Lord. Your body is where I reside (temple of the Holy Ghost); however, you can, and many times do choose to ignore my Spirit and follow your own way. This is dangerous, and the consequences are great.

You attempt to change on your own, but you were not created to handle such loads. I created you to depend on me for direction, instruction, guidance, and all that you need to live an abundant life. Keep in mind that nothing in the kingdom is automatic. I, in my sovereignty, chose to give you free will; this means you can choose life or death. What you sow, you will surely reap. If you sow to the flesh, of the flesh you reap corruption. If you sow to the spirit, then you will reap life everlasting. Therefore, the world cannot see me in you. You are very much like the world. I have given you the grace to become more like me each day that you choose to fellowship with me.

Time with me is never wasted, but you must seek me with your whole heart. You must choose to do things my way and not follow your opinion, comparing yourself with others. The standard for living is not another man, but the standard of living is found in my word. Will you not allow me to grow you up? You could not remain an infant in the natural; why do you not want to grow up in the spirit? If you continue to want your way instead of mine, you remain immature as an infant throws temper tantrum to have his/her way. Allow me to invade your life; I only come when invited. Decide to yield your human spirit to my Spirit within. Only as you feed your spirit with my word will you have the right spirit in operation. Stop manipulating my word for your convenience. Ask me and I will teach you the truth. Remember, I am love. Anything that is not motivated by love is not me.

Message to the Five-Fold Ministry

Study *and* do your best to present yourself to God approved,
a workman [tested by trial] who has no reason to be ashamed,
accurately handling *and* skillfully teaching the word of truth.

—2 Timothy 2:15 (AMP)

So Christ himself gave the apostles, the prophets, the
evangelists, the pastors and teachers, to equip his people for
works of service, so that the body of Christ may be built up.

—Ephesians 4:11 (NIV)

I have called you and chosen you to carry my mantle of truth. You are my messengers and carriers of the sword of the Spirit. Spend time with me and my word so I can give you my vision for this hour. You cannot speak what you have not heard, and you cannot share with others that which you do not have.

You are called for the maturing of the Body and to edify the Body, not to make a name for yourself. I am building my many-membered army, but you are on the frontline; therefore, remain diligent in spending time with me daily. You are under attack only because you are on the frontline. Even as the enemy struck me at the cross and my sheep (disciples) scattered, he has not changed his actions, but he is still striking leaders through deception and division.

Keep in mind that he was defeated by me then and remains defeated now. However, you must enforce his defeat by confessing and living my word, believing my word, and placing it as first authority in your life. "So *submit to* [the authority of] *God.* Resist the devil [stand firm against him] and he will flee from you" (James 4:7, AMP). Prepare your heart daily; don't follow the trends of man, but allow me to give you revelations and a fresh word that can only come through time spent in my presence and in my word. Be careful to avoid your interpretation. But I am a teacher; ask me and I will instruct you so that you can instruct the people with a clear conscious.

> Preach the word; be prepared in season and out of season; correct, rebuke and encourage—with great patience and careful instruction. For the time will come when people will not put up with sound doctrine. Instead, to suit their own desires, they will gather around them a great number of teachers to say what their itching ears want to hear. They will turn their ears away from the truth and turn aside to myths. (2 Timothy 4:2–4, NIV)

Be at peace in seeking and pleasing me above all else. Refuse to be a man-pleaser, but seek my will and my way in all things. Time with me will keep you grounded and open to my heart so that you do not err. My word and my Spirit will always agree. I will never tell you to do something that contradicts my word.

Don't use my word to manipulate and control, for I weigh the motives and the heart. A spiritual revolution must begin in the private time with me, so when you meet with people in the world or in my house, time with me will be noticeable in everything you say and do. Allow my grace, my mercy, and my love to consume you, and my glory will come.

Message to Intercessors

I looked for someone among them who would build up *the*
wall and *stand* before me *in the gap* on behalf of *the* land
so I would not have to destroy it, but I found no one.

—Ezekiel 22:30 (NIV)

Finally, be strong in the Lord and in his mighty power. Put on
the full armor of God, so that you can take your stand against
the devil's schemes… And pray in the Spirit on all occasions
with all kinds of prayers and requests. With this in mind, be
alert and always keep on praying for all the Lord's people.

—Ephesians 6:10–11, 18 (NIV)

The time that you have spent with me in private in your closet
have not gone unnoticed. Yet, even as I needed someone to stand in
the gap on behalf of Jerusalem, so now I call you to cry out for the
nation and the nations of the world. Many of my people have lost
their way, and the trends of the day and culture are swallowing them
up with distractions. Watch your words and your heart, for I hasten
to perform my word (not your interpretation of my word). Allow my
Spirit to instruct you and guide you, but stand as a watchman on the
wall for this nation.

The time is short, and I have much that is yet to be done, but
I have chosen to work through you. Though you are in the back-
ground, you kindle the fire before the meeting starts. Did you not
know that spiritual things cannot be naturally discerned? That is why
many have been blindsided. The ills of the nation are being handled

by natural means, but they have a spiritual root. Destroy the root and the fruit will die. Be led by my Spirit, and be not guilty of vain repetitions. For you already know that I desire your best and the best for my nations. However, you know that it is not automatic; it is a choice.

> When I shut up the heavens so that there is no rain, or command locusts to devour the land or send a plague among my people, if my people, who are called by my name, will humble themselves and pray and seek my face and turn from their wicked ways, then I will hear from heaven, and I will forgive their sin and will heal their land. Now my eyes will be open and my ears attentive to the prayers offered in this place. (2 Chronicles 7:13–15, NIV)

Resist the temptation to perform in your own strength and accept my grace to do what I have set you aside to do. Keep your mouth from speaking evil of those who have wronged you. Be quick to forgive and walk in love so that your prayers are not hindered.

> Therefore, confess your sins to one another [your false steps, your offenses], and pray for one another, that you may be healed *and* restored. *The heartfelt and* persistent prayer of a righteous man (believer) can accomplish much [when put into action and made effective by God—it is dynamic and can have tremendous power]. The heartfelt *and* persistent prayer of a righteous man (believer) can accomplish much [when put into action and made effective by God—it is dynamic and can have tremendous power]. (James 5:16, AMP)

For you are the watchman on the wall, taking the city, the nation, the world for me. Your private time seeking me on behalf of others will saturate the atmosphere and prepare the hearts of those who need to hear my voice; be ready to receive the truth of my word. Don't take my presence for granted. Pray in the Spirit to get my heart. Refuse to die the slow death of indecision. Decide today to do it my way and not your way.

> Let the [spoken] word of Christ have its home within you [dwelling in your heart and mind— permeating every aspect of your being] as you teach [spiritual things] and admonish *and* train one another with all wisdom, *singing* psalms and *hymns* and spiritual *songs* with thankfulness in your hearts to God. (Colossians 3:16, AMP)

Let the spiritual revolution begin with each of you, and carry that fire into every sphere of influence that you enter. Watch me, for I will confirm my word with signs following when my people decide to do things my way and not adhere to divisive tactics of the enemy and trends of the culture.

Message to Unbelievers

The Lord is not slow in keeping his promise, as some understand slowness. Instead he is patient with you, not wanting anyone to perish, but everyone to come to repentance.

—2 Peter 3:9 (NIV)

I love you with an everlasting love. I know that you have resisted me only because you cannot see my love for you. If only you knew it was for you that I died. You would know how special you are to me. You refuse me because you have a false representation of me in the earth. If you really knew me, you would never want to go back to the things of the world.

I created you in my image and after my likeness. That emptiness that you feel, the need to fill a void, is your spirit crying out for me. Nothing that you accomplish or do in this life will meet that need because I created you to fellowship with me. I am not angry at you. I have sent my messengers to share my love, but they are so wrapped up in their own opinions that they refuse to be an instrument of my love.

Don't fret for I have those who will do things my way. They will seek my truth and not the fables of men handed down from generations. It is "my truth" that sets men free. I am still here, and I am the same God yesterday, today, and forever. I have not changed; it is my people that have changed. Yet I will always have those that love me and will obey me. You will know them by their love for one another.

Don't be too hard on my children, for as you were once an infant and grew to be an adult, so too it is with spiritual maturity. I have children that only know about me, but they still are mine. You see, it has nothing to do with performance. It has to do with making the choice and decision to allow me to be Lord and Savior of your life.

I will send messengers to you, but you must understand that I do nothing by force. I have given you "free will" to accept me or reject me. Your decision does not change my love for you. For I know that satan has blinded the eyes of those who have not accepted me. When you open your heart to my word and allow me to reveal myself to you, I will make myself known in a way that only I can do.

You ask, "Why do I need you?" You must know that the decision that was made by Adam at creation impacted humanity forever. Man was created in my image and likeness, and therefore he knew no evil. However, when he chose to disobey me and obey satan instead, satan became his god instead of me. He then lost fellowship with me and took on the nature of satan. Everyone born into the world from that time is born with a sin nature because of Adams actions, even as decisions of the president of the USA impacts its citizens.

Although I defeated satan at Cavalry and stripped him of his power and authority, men are still choosing to listen to his deception and lies. Listen to my word and trust me to be your Lord and Savior. I will fill the void in your life and recreate your spirit with my Spirit. As you spend time with me in my word and prayer, you will come to know me for who I am. For I am the way, the truth, and the life; no man comes to the Father except by me. Let me have your heart (all of it), and I will never leave you nor forsake you. You will learn of me and my unconditional love for you.

Conclusion

"By this everyone will *know* that *you are my disciples*, if *you* love one another."

—John 13:35 (NIV)

As I began the journey to understand my life as an African American Christian woman in 2012, I was a very wounded and bitter person. Despite my feeling, my heart knew that God was not the author of confusion; He hates division, and He certainly disapproves of hatred and disobedience.

While I did not intentionally disobey God, I had allowed the circumstances of my life to cloud my perspective on God's love for me. Although I felt that my excuses for holding unforgiveness in my heart for the white race was valid and justified, God kept reminding me that He had paid the price for the sin of the world with the blood of his only Son.

If I was to experience the manifestation of God's goodness in my life, I had to choose to forgive everyone who had wronged and hurt me. I had to choose to love them despite the fact that I knew that I was hated by many (only because of the color of my skin). As I looked at the history of my ancestors, I am embarrassed to say that I had allowed shame to take control of my thoughts. The idea that a human being could be treated as property was more than my heart could take. Not to mention that many people used God's word as a means to justify their wrong.

If slavery had ended with the abolition of slavery, I would probably have been fine. However, the difference between the children of Israel being freed from Egyptian slavery and American slavery was:

- Although Joseph was betrayed by his brothers and was sold into slavery, Israel ended up in Egypt by choice. Joseph had become prime minister of Egypt, and there was a famine in the land where his father lived. When his brothers visited Egypt to ask for food, they did not know that Joseph had lived and was the person that gave permission for their food. Later, Joseph invited his family to join him in Egypt. They chose to join Joseph in Egypt to avoid the famine. They were not herded over on slave ships with shackles on their ankles and necks like cattle as African slaves.

- Jealousy caused Pharaoh to begin to fear the Israelites. Joseph had died before his family went into slavery. Greed prompted American slavery. Pride and Fear kept it alive.

- The exodus of the Israelites from Egypt left them with great Egyptian possessions; American slaves left with nothing.

- God miraculously delivered Israel from Pharaoh, killing an entire army. God miraculously delivered American slaves by raising up people who fought against slavery. Unfortunately, slave owners who were responsible for the laws of the land wrapped slavery in a different wrapper within the law. These laws still exist today; although the wrappers have changed, the residue of slavery is portrayed in racism.

I can hear God saying, "Let my people go!" He has extended grace again and again, but we must never frustrate the grace of God or use his grace as an occasion to sin. To my white Christian brothers and sisters who feel superior to me and hate me because of the color my skin, I pray that God will soften your heart to see the truth of his word. You are without excuse even if you were taught wrong. "My people are destroyed from lack of knowledge. Because you have rejected knowledge, I also reject you as my priests; because you have ignored the law of your God, I also will ignore your children" (Hosea 4:6, NIV). To my black Christian brothers and sisters who have accepted the lie and treat other races better than you treat those who look like you, I would ask you renew your mind with the word of

God on who you really are (In Christ). "We saw the Nephilim there (the descendants of Anak come from the Nephilim). We seemed like *grasshoppers* in our own eyes, and we looked the same to them" (Numbers 13:33, NIV).

This journey is not over as I continue to search for truth. I have come to understand racism better. I know that satan is the author of confusion and division, but he has no power except the power that we give him. I choose to love my brothers and sisters. I choose to forgive those that have wronged me and my ancestors, and I choose to see myself the way the Creator sees me. Of one thing I am confident: God created me in his image and after his likeness and everything he created was good (including me and my black skin). "I praise you because I am *fearfully and wonderfully* made; your works are wonderful, I know that full well" (Psalm 139:14, NIV).

> By this everyone will *know* that *you are my disciples*, if *you* love one another." (John 13:35, NIV)

Closing Prayer

But you are a chosen people, a *royal priesthood*, a holy nation,
God's special possession, that you may declare the praises of
him who called you out of darkness into his wonderful light.

—1 Peter 2:9 (NIV)

Father God, in the name of Jesus Christ my Lord, Savior, and King, I honor You above every name that is named. I honor your word above my opinion, my experiences, and the circumstances of my life. I exalt your name now and always. At your name, I surrender to the wisdom of God above my own wisdom or the wisdom of man.

Father, your word says if we lack wisdom, we could ask You, the giver of all wisdom, and You would give it to us. We in America, especially the Body of Christ, need your wisdom on the matter of racism. Open the eyes of those whose eyes have been blinded by satan; soften the hearts of those who know the truth but refuse to yield to the truth. Forgive me for not demonstrating nor experiencing the joy unspeakable and full of glory that Peter describes in 1 Peter 1:8. I truly want to know Christ and be known of Christ, even as Paul prayed to know You in Philippians 3:7–10. I pray for your Body of Christ the same prayers that Paul prayed for the churches at Ephesus and Colossae:

I keep asking that the God of our Lord Jesus
Christ, the glorious Father, may give His Body
the Spirit of wisdom and revelation, so that we
may know him better. I pray that the eyes of
your heart may be enlightened in order that

we may know the hope to which he has called us, the riches of his glorious inheritance in his holy people, and his incomparably great power for us who believe. That power is the same as the mighty strength he exerted when he raised Christ from the dead and seated him at his right hand in the heavenly realms, far above all rule and authority, power and dominion, and every name that is invoked, not only in the present age but also in the one to come. And God placed all things under his feet and appointed him to be head over everything for the church, which is his body, the fullness of him who fills everything in every way. (Ephesians 1:17–23, NIV)

I kneel before the Father, from whom every family[a] in heaven and on earth derives its name. I pray that out of his glorious riches he may strengthen His Body with power through his Spirit in our inner being, so that Christ may dwell in our hearts through faith. And I pray that we, being rooted and established in love, may have power, together with all the Lord's holy people, to grasp how wide and long and high and deep is the love of Christ, and to know this love that surpasses knowledge—that we may be filled to the measure of all the fullness of God.

Now to him who is able to do immeasurably more than all we ask or imagine, according to his power that is at work within us, to him be glory in the church and in Christ Jesus throughout all generations, for ever and ever! Amen. (Ephesians 3:14–21, NIV)

I continually ask God to fill His Body with the knowledge of his will through all the wisdom and understanding that the Spirit gives, so that we may live a life worthy of the Lord and please him in every way: bearing fruit in every good work, growing in the knowledge of God, being strengthened with all power according to his glorious might so that we may have great endurance and patience, and giving joyful thanks to the Father, who has qualified us[f] to share in the inheritance of his holy people in the kingdom of light. For he has rescued us from the dominion of darkness and brought us into the kingdom of the Son he loves, in whom we have redemption, the forgiveness of sins. (Colossians 1:9–14, NIV)

Lord, only You can heal the broken and wounded hearts that have scars left by the stench of slavery, oppression, and racism. Only You, Lord God, can give us the grace to love one another the way you instructed us to love, and see one another through your eyes.

Help us to remember that we are not fighting people or a natural battle, but a spiritual battle. Remind us that spiritual things cannot be discerned naturally, nor can a spiritual battle be handled by natural means. Help us to see the same tricks that have been used throughout history to divide God's people are being used today. I recognize that time is short, and You need a people who will relinquish their right to be white or black and instead stand bold and strong in the blood of the Lord Jesus as children of the Most High God.

You are our strength, Lord. We choose to trust You and acknowledge You, knowing that You will direct our path. We know that what is impossible with man is possible with You. You said if we commit whatever we do to You, You would establish your plan for us. We choose to meditate in your word day and night and be a doer of your word; we choose to refrain from murmuring and complaining. Father, we choose to walk in love and forgive with your grace.

Father, raise up those serious believers and intercessors who want your will above all else in this world. Intercessors who know who they are in You, are known by you, and know how to enforce what You have already done for us. Help us to walk in the authority that You reclaimed for us on Cavalry.

Your word said blessed is the nation whose God is the Lord. We decree that you are the God of the United States of America and its people. You have instructed us that we should have no other god before you, so we yield to that truth. We recognize that You allow us to choose, so we do not force our belief on anyone, but in love give us the wisdom to share the "Good News" of the Gospel of Jesus Christ to every man. Help us to find our true identity in You and not what the world says about us.

> And they sang a new song, saying: "You are worthy to take the scroll and to open its seals, because you were slain, and with your blood you purchased for God persons from *every tribe* and language and people and *nation*. (Revelation 5:9, NIV)

Show us the way, Father, and help us to walk in your truth. Your way is the only way, and we choose you all over again. Help us to continue this prayer in our private time as we pray your perfect will in the Spirit. Help us to accept your grace for our lives and extend grace to others as we seek to know you better. In Jesus's name.

About the Author

D r. Margaret Gray Robinson is the fourth of twelve children born to the later Rev. and Mrs. John M. Gray in Birmingham, Alabama, during the Civil Rights movement. She is divorced and has two adult sons.

Dr. Robinson is a retired educator with a PhD from the University of Alabama. She is a born-again, spirit-filled Christian whose heart's desire is for the Body of Christ (all inclusive), to experience kingdom living here on earth.

Dr. Robinson is a graduate of Ever Increasing Word Ministry, Kingdom School of Ministry, and Rhema Bible Training College. She is the author of *From the Heart of God: My Bride Prepare* (2008) and the companion book to *USA and Racial Divide: Lord Heal Me and Heal our Land* entitled *Struggle Without: Struggle Within* (under publication). Her greatest passion is ministering the love of God and positioning God's people to an intimate relationship with the Father through Jesus Christ and love for one another. This book was commissioned by God in answer to a prayer about racism. God's answer was clear: "It cannot be Accomplished by the Marches of the 1960's, but by a Spiritual Revolution" (i.e., men's hearts must change).